The Nurturing Teacher

Managing the Stress of Caring

KJERSTI VANSLYKE-BRIGGS

Forward by Stephanie Paterson

Rowman & Littlefield Education

A Division of
ROWMAN & LITTLEFIELD PUBLISHERS, INC.
Walnut Creek • Lanham • New York • Toronto • Plymouth, UK

Published by Rowman & Littlefield Education
A division of Rowman & Littlefield Publishers, Inc.
A wholly owned subsidary of The Rowman & Littlefield Publishing Group, Inc.
4501 Forbes Boulevard, Suite 200, Lanham, Maryland 20706
http://www.rowmaneducation.com

Estover Road, Plymouth PL6 7PY, United Kingdom

British Library Cataloguing in Publication Information Available

Library of Congress Cataloging-in-Publication Data
VanSlyke-Briggs, Kjersti.
  The nurturing teacher : managing the stress of caring / Kjersti VanSlyke-Briggs.
    p. cm.
  ISBN 978-1-60709-397-8 (cloth : alk. paper) — ISBN 978-1-60709-398-5 (pbk. : alk. paper) — ISBN 978-1-60709-399-2 (electronic)
    1. Teachers—Job stress. 2. Teachers—Mental health. 3. Burn out (Psychology)—Prevention. 4. Teaching—Psychological aspects. I. Title.
LB2840.2.V36 2010
371.1001'9—dc22   2009040363

∞ ™ The paper used in this publication meets the minimum requirements of American National Standard for Information Sciences—Permanence of Paper for Printed Library Materials, ANSI/NISO Z39.48-1992.

Printed in the United States of America

For my community of caring: my parents who fostered my love for education and encouraged me to go to college and keep going until I received my doctorate, my first principal who told me to just do what was good for kids and encouraged me to nurture my students, my husband for his patience as I dealt with the stress of getting this book into your hands, and my daughter who often is my inspiration.

Contents

Foreword

Some days when I come home from teaching I feel physically flattened and emotionally bereft. I carry home a backpack full of papers from four writing classes and know they will not make it out of the bag. My heavy sense of duty confronts my empty interior. There is no juice left. The well is empty. I am consumed with a fatigue that surpasses the simple challenge of not having had enough sleep. I am emotionally, spiritually, physically depleted, and I know I have to go back tomorrow and do it again.

I think of the poem "Sweet Darkness," by David Whyte that begins,

> When your eyes are tired
> the world is tired also.
> When your vision has gone
> no part of the world can find you.[1]

I am reminded that the fatigue that attacks me at my core is as much about perception as it is about a hunger for rest and a deep desire for the world to slow down just a little. The poem ends,

> You must learn one thing.
> The world was made to be free in.
> Give up all the other worlds
> except the one to which you belong.

> Sometimes it takes darkness and the sweet
> confinement of your aloneness
> to learn
> anything or anyone
> that does not bring you alive
> is too small for you.[2]

I started to teach composition twelve years ago and although the dark, bleak days still visit me, they are fewer and farther between, if only, in part because I hold Whyte's lines as an ongoing challenge: "anything or anyone / that does not bring you alive / is too small for you."[3] I have learned that it takes conscious effort to keep the spirit alive in this profession.

If any of this sounds familiar, if you feel weary and beleaguered, you will find Kjersti B. VanSlyke-Briggs's book a gem, because she understands the devastating dissipation of energy and the slow, insidious loss of self that happens when work-related stress becomes a way of life. This exciting study is part ethnography, part self-help, part *ethnofiction*, which she describes as "the blurring of genres and presentation of data through creative writing," part history and part call-to-action. It's a mental health manifesto for emotionally, physically, spiritually famished teachers at all stages of a career.

VanSlyke-Briggs etymologically traces the roots of the term *stress* back to the field of engineering. She places her study in a historical context that helps to explain the feminization of teaching. One of her original contributions to scholarship is to coin a unique phrase to describe the invisible (but all too common) factors in teacher burnout—*nurturance suffering*: a form of stress that is a result of the emotional ties to students. As she notes, the "emotional labor" of teaching is not something that is often talked about in teacher education or a preservice teaching course.[4]

Viewing education through a *sociocultural* lens, and through cinematic and fictional representations of "super" teachers, VanSlyke-Briggs shows how damaging cultural myths get perpetuated. She offers a series of provocative case studies of individual teachers who suffer from different manifestations of *burnout*, defined as a loss of idealism and enthusiasm for work.[5] She highlights the prevalence of this pernicious phenomenon, mapping the fault lines in both the outer educational landscape and the inner landscape. She argues, in short, that too many teachers are isolated. They suffer from a loss of control that comes from having too many external mandates divorced from the realities of classroom life. They perceive their struggle as personal failing—"there must be something wrong with me."

In this book VanSlyke-Briggs builds on the work of writers like Parker Palmer, *The Courage to Teach* and Mary Rose O'Reilley, *The Garden at Night: Burnout and Breakdown in the Teaching Life.*[6] She understands "the most practical thing we can achieve in any kind of work is insight into what is happening inside us as we do it. The more familiar we are with our inner terrain, the more surefooted our teaching—and living—becomes."[7] To accomplish this, VanSlyke-Briggs offers concrete steps and actions that we all might take, such as keeping a stress journal or diary, and she also advocates for large-scale programs for teachers to learn to address and cope with debilitating levels of stress.

In the Consider This sections of this book, VanSlyke-Briggs poses thoughtful questions to reflect upon and ask yourself. For example, she asks, "Do you have a support network that you can share with?" I am fortunate to be part of the National Writing Project, and at our local site we have, as VanSlyke-Briggs recommends, created a Ning network. One of our forum discussions centers on the topic of self-renewal. The facilitator jump-started our online dialogue with the following invitation: "Many of us are suffering from lack of balance in our life. We need to hear what you're doing so we can learn from you!" As of this date, there are ten postings. One teacher started taking an oil painting class. Another teacher says she's learned to pause before saying yes to things that will require a lot of her time. Another takes the time "to do the Jumble in the morning," to walk, take a hot bath, read for leisure, go horseback riding, sew, and garden. "Connect with colleagues," VanSlyke-Briggs recommends, to combat the "pioneer ethic" that leaves us all isolated in teaching silos.

This is a timely book because there is little doubt that teachers and students are hurting. I hear stories directly and indirectly every day. However, we do seem to be at a *tipping point* because there are more and more signs of a new cultural awareness that the physiological and psychological effects of stress, and stress-related illnesses, quite simply kills.[8] Two days ago, I received an e-mail update from my health insurance provider announcing a new "Emotional Wellness Program" as part of the yearlong healthy lifestyle program. This is just one sign of the tipping point I refer to and the cultural zeitgeist that VanSlyke-Briggs has tapped into. The insurance companies are now investing in online educational materials to increase clients' awareness of wellness behaviors and habits of mind. They know that while there is a great cost personally to individuals who are burned out, there is also a great financial cost. Like VanSlyke-Briggs, they utilize breakthrough research coming out of the field of positive psychology. Instead of taking the traditional DSM deficit approach to illness they are taking a strengths-based approach of assessing what's working and building a life from there.

Recently, at a book signing in San Francisco, author Jill Dearman said she used to work on a "Hear to Help Hotline,"[9] and in training for this work the facilitator mentioned the worst callers were the "help rejecting complainers." This particular species have a "yeah, but . . ." for every solution. If you're a help-rejecting complainer this book will probably not be for you, for it calls for proactive behavior, for self-responsibility and awareness coupled with action. I think it is exciting that VanSlyke-Briggs turns the action research lens inward to study the root causes of burnout and then highlights techniques for cultivating wellness and finding stress-relieving outlets. I like that she uses the cycle of inquiry, so familiar to teacher researchers, as a way of thinking through crisis. In this book, you will learn how to create a management plan. Developing self-care plans is incorporated into course work for social workers and medical doctors; it is unfortunate that the field of education has been slow to explicitly address this same need in our profession, but VanSlyke-Briggs fills this desperate gap.

I have read that "teaching is one of those jobs that could fill up every waking minute of every day" and "teaching is a paradox because it is the type of job that is impossible to figure out."[10] There is no formula. There is no settling the score. Ours is a kind of work marked by perpetual process, perpetual ambiguity, and not-knowing. What this book offers is a rich array of tactical strategies and habits of mind for living in the paradox without being burned up. While reading this book, you'll come to see that "it's not what happens *to* you, it's what happens *in* you, what you do with what happens to you—in your work and your relationships—that really matters."[11] If you're hunting for hope, you'll find it here.

Stephanie Paterson is an associate professor of English at California State University, Stanislaus, where she teaches graduate and undergraduate courses in writing, specializing in rhetoric and composition. She is codirector of the Great Valley Writing Project. Her most recent work includes "Friday Writes: An Exercise in the Believing Game," published in JAEPL *(2009–2010) guest edited by Peter Elbow, and "Four Antidotes to Burnout and Breakdown in the Teaching Life," published in* The English Record, *guest edited by Tim Fredrick, Spring 2009.*

NOTES

1. David Whyte, *The House of Belonging* (Langley, Wash.: Many Rivers Press, 1997), 23. © Many Rivers Press, Langley, Washington. Printed with permission from Many Rivers Press, www.davidwhyte.com.

2. Ibid.

3. Ibid.

4. Arlie Hochschild, *The Managed Heart: Commercialization of Human Feeling* (Berkeley: University of California Press, 2003).

5. Chris McCarthy and Terri Wood, "Understanding and Preventing Teacher Burnout," *ERIC Digest.* December 2002, at www.ericsp.org/pages/digests/02-03.pdf.

6. Parker J. Palmer, *The Courage to Teach: Exploring the Inner Landscape of a Teacher's Life* (San Francisco: Jossey-Bass Publishers, 1998); Mary Rose O'Reilley, *The Garden at Night: Burnout and Breakdown in the Teaching Life* (Portsmouth, N.H.: Boynton/Cook Publishers, 2005).

7. Palmer, *The Courage to Teach*, 5.

8. Malcolm Gladwell, *The Tipping Point: How Little Things Can Make a Big Difference* (Boston: Back Bay Books, 2002).

9. Jill Dearman, *Band the Keys: Four Steps to a Lifelong Writing Practice* (New York: Alpha Books, 2009).

10. Nancy Mack, "Energy and Enthusiasm: Don't Start the School Year without Them," *English Journal* 98(1):18–25.

11. Phil Cousineau, *Stoking the Creative Fires: 9 Ways to Rekindle Passion and Imagination* (San Francisco: Conari Press, 2008), 146–47.

Preface: The Importance of Nurturing

My interest in a study of stress related to teaching and in particular in relation to nurturing teaching came about as a combination of events. My teaching in an alternative school coincided with doctoral courses in education. During my years of teaching at this school, I found myself with high stress levels and believed it was a result of not being able to "fix" the problems my students had in their lives. At the same time, I came across a reading that spoke of teachers as nurturers. Certainly, I was a nurturer of my students; at least that is how I came to see myself. Contrary to the images that are evoked when hearing the word *nurturing*, I was not in blissful harmony with my environment and able to mentor and guide students with ease and smiles. Instead, I was stressed out, and very cranky. Unable to manage my stress effectively, I feared what many early-career teachers fear: burnout.

One student in particular stands out from this period of time. Georgia was an eleventh grade student who I had taught the year before. She routinely came in to eat lunch in my room and chat about what was going on in her life. Georgia had never had it easy in her life and at this point had been living for several years with her grandmother. It wasn't long into the school year when she learned the news that her grandmother was very ill and was diagnosed with cancer. Georgia suddenly found herself in a very adult world as she was responsible for taking her grandmother to her cancer treatments, paying bills, and performing other household management tasks.

Several months later, her grandmother died and Georgia was alone in the world. We spent many tearful lunches throughout this tumultuous time as she looked for some sort of guidance. Georgia's mother came back into her life when she was planning the funeral; shortly after the funeral services, her mother began to contest the will, which left the house and car to Georgia. In an effort to prove she could maintain a financial balance to pay the bills, Georgia soon quit school to work full-time.

This struggle to try and help Georgia lasted well into the winter of that school year and when she finally resolved to quit school, I felt as if I had failed her. Because she was eighteen, Georgia could legally quit school, and although she was torn, she felt she had no choice but to quit in order to maintain a place to live. No amount of intervention on my part was able to help her and when she left the school, I realized I could not fix this situation or help improve it from my position as a teacher. Georgia was forced into the role of an adult, long before she was ready and long before any student should be asked to take on this responsibility.

The rest of that year followed with similar scenarios of students who came to me with problems I could do nothing to solve from my position of teacher. I was only able to provide an ear for students to share their pain and only ineffective words of support. Shortly thereafter, I encountered a text by Valerie Walkerdine (1992) that discussed the positioning of women as nurturers and the metaphor of teacher as container for student concerns. I projected this interpretation onto my own life and my emotional struggles over Georgia. As a result of this connection of theory to practice, I began looking into the relationship of teaching and the development of stress in teachers.

I had the opportunity to test out some of my ideas at my alternative high school. It was during this time that I first began to talk to my peer teachers and hear their stories of care-related stress. Much like my own story, many of the focus teachers I spoke with for this project had particular students they connected to emotionally and who in attempting to help found themselves stressed as a result. Again, similar to my experiences, it appeared they had not developed coping strategies for dealing with this stress as a result of emotional labor. Others were stressed due to a sense of a loss of control and another factor contributing to stress that continued to emerge was a lack of connectedness with colleagues. While many of the teachers I focused on were fairly new teachers and had worked in public schools less than five years, others were tenured and practiced teachers. The similarities in their stress levels were not something I had expected. One individual I worked with at length had taught for over ten years and had a background in guidance counseling. Of the many teachers I spoke with, this was one of the few who had a concrete plan in place for dealing with the stress of teaching and nurturing. The case studies that follow in chapter 3 incorporate the stories of each of these teachers.

Over time, in my own teaching, I began to develop some coping mechanisms, but I was not happy with the result. I found myself pulling away from students emotionally and this was not an effective strategy for me personally. What I wanted was to understand why teachers (and in particular female teachers) connect with students emotionally and how to better do that work, which is so important for the student. The coping mechanisms that I developed for myself have carried over to my current practices and can be used to help cope with a variety of stress instigators. As I continued my own investigations into teacher stress, I found myself speaking about it both formally and informally in teacher gatherings such as at professional organization meetings and conferences. In talking with other teachers from across my own state and across the country, I continued to hear echoed my own complaints. New teachers in particular were quick to point out that they had never prepared for this and were at a loss with how to cope. More tenured teachers appeared frustrated but resigned to the belief that it came with the job.

Armed with more knowledge about nurturing-related stress and other job-related stressors, I feel that I could have been a stronger person and more present for my students early in my career. In my time with the teachers I spoke with in order to gain material for this book, I learned to improve my own interactions with students while still preserving self. This book does not set out to define all the answers to the connection between stress and emotional labor; it does set out to explore that connection and examine how we as teachers may manage our own stress in order to better fulfill the needs of our students. It is my hope that readers will be able to identify enclosed case studies that resonate with their own lives. Perhaps by viewing these case studies (composites of several teachers), and by practicing some of the stress-relieving techniques that follow, teachers can prevent burnout or emotional distancing from their students.

Introduction

It is no surprise that teachers experience much stress throughout the course of a typical career. Working closely with students, many teachers become emotionally connected to students and worry about them. Teachers also have mountains of paperwork that never seem to diminish, a litany of standards to meet, test scores to keep up, professional development hours to accumulate, and a career place that is ever changing. Teachers come to the field often expecting to experience stress. They assume that stress is part of the job and an element that must just be tolerated. This is simply not true. We each experience different forms of stress and every person has a different way of reacting to stress, but there is no rule that states teachers must have it as part of the daily events.

This text will focus on the various forms of stress and in particular on nurturance suffering: a form of stress that is a result of the emotional ties to students. The rate of teacher attrition is often noted in reporting trends on teachers, and statistics reach soaring numbers such as in claims that in urban centers in particular up to half of the teachers who enter the field leave within five years. According to McCann et al., "Nearly one in three teachers who begin the profession leaves within the first three years."[1] It is no wonder that when facing so much stress in so many forms teachers reach burnout and leave teaching. We need to better manage our stress and to care for each other. Teachers need to look out for each other and our students in a community with a climate of caring. One pattern identified in those teachers likely to stay in the profession is that they share their experiences with their peers rather than harbor those experiences as personal hurdles.[2]

Teachers bring their whole history to the practice. This sociocultural look at teaching asks us to consider our own background and the influence society and media have had on the attitudes we bring to the field. Given the plethora of Hollywood films and television dramas in which a teacher is painted as a hero/savior, it is easy to understand why many young people new to the field feel as if they are out to save the world and later feel as if they are not up to the challenge. Team this sense of inevitable failure with poor working conditions and the statistics on teachers leaving the field become even clearer. Many young teachers also have to fight off the "ghost teacher" who lingers around their classrooms. This ghost teacher is a collection of all the great teachers the novice has had in the past. This collection of teacher images is difficult to live up to, especially when the novice romanticizes the memories of past teachers and was not present to see that teacher frustrated at the end of the day just like everyone else.

We should not let go of those images, however, but should use them realistically to fuel our careers. We can still be hopeful about our classrooms and try to live up to an ideal as long as we can balance that with a healthy respect for our challenges. It is not a failure that a favorite student drops out of school, but a challenge that was unable to be prevented. It is not a failure that all the thematic essays were not graded by Monday, but a challenge that time could not stop for us to finish. Teachers have great potential for influencing the lives of students and past challenges should not prevent future attempts. Sonia Nieto in her text *What Keeps Teachers Going* notes that teachers are agents for change "whose words and deeds change lives and mold futures. . . . Teachers *can* and *do* exert a great deal of power and influence in the lives of their students."[3] Those moments of success need to be recorded as a reminder that what teachers do counts, and yes, often there is a chance to make a difference.

Nieto includes the comments of one of the teachers she interviewed for the book and that teacher, Junia, stated, "I feel I am the protector. My room is their haven. They're safe here."[4] This is just how many of the teachers I interviewed who experienced nurturance suffering felt. They considered it a mark of an excellent teacher to care emotionally for students as did I in my own experience, but it was that same level of care that when unbalanced and when unrealistically applied led to stress and burnout.

This culture of caring as a mark of good teaching comes to even novice teachers. In working with my own student teachers, I ask them at the close of each placement about the challenges and successes they experienced. I also ask about how they managed their stress and what helped them continue to want to be a teacher. Just this last spring, one student, Celia, responded, "I love teaching. It just makes me happy. The kids are hilarious and it warms my heart, as corny as that may sound, to see them learn and grow into young adults. I feel like it is an honor for me to be their teacher. They trust me to be their role model and guide." Another student teacher, Christopher, noted that he often felt like a nurturer in the classroom because he connected with students. He noted the following example: "I had a student who came from a broken home and was actually staying in a shelter. She would come and vent to me sometimes and I would try to offer her reasonable advice and encouragement. I went out of my way to make sure her needs were met, but I didn't let it jeopardize the standards I had set for the rest of the students." Both Celia and Christopher as well as most of my other student teachers found an emotional caring for students to be not only a mark of good teaching, but also a point to be proud of. With this level of commitment to the whole child comes stress, and without healthy management tools of this stress, these early career teachers are at high risk for burnout and in danger of leaving the profession.

Others who do not subscribe to this understanding of the role of teachers as nurturer are uncomfortable with the word *care* and fear it interferes with the delivery of content. *Care* simply means to be invested in students and their education as it applies to the whole child. How can we as teachers instruct content when we first do not attend to the emotional needs of students? This is not about being a friend or a mother to students, but about bringing in those qualities to best nurture students to understanding. McCann et al. note that a "sense of duty to help young people"[5] is also a key identifying factor of those teachers who may have longevity in the field. This task is often difficult and brings on more stress. I will look at this in more detail in chapter 1 and throughout this text.

Reciprocal caring often helps alleviate teacher stress and reminds teachers of the value of their work. It is these instances, however small, in which a student or other faculty members display caring toward the teacher. A thank you or a gesture of appreciation or care for the teacher can go a long way to help balance out stress from nurturance suffering. It can also help balance out the sense of loneliness that comes from teaching. Although surrounded by people all day, teachers are rarely in meaningful contact with other adults. As Nieto points out, the few adult encounters that do occur within a day are often superficial.[6] I agree with Nieto that teaching should not be a solitary or private work ethic. Teachers need to share their experiences and build meaningful and supportive relationships with colleagues. This is especially true for student teachers and new teachers as they have yet to fully understand the dynamics of the school building. Mentoring programs if implemented well can make a big difference in eliminating this sense of isolation.

Although many teachers live on hope that situations will improve and stress will lesson, it isn't always enough and stress management should be put into place. As one of my recent student teachers put it, "I just try to suck it up [stress] and get through because at this point, everything I have done has been worth it to finally be a real teacher." Without a stress plan, hope can only carry a person so far. This book is designed to help teachers first identify the root causes of stress, recognize their stress reactions and triggers, and create a management plan for coping with stress in order to continue the work in a healthy way. This book should be viewed as a tool or guide, but will require the reader to actively engage with the text and be reflexive about his or her own habits and practices.

NOTES

1. Thomas M. McCann, Larry R. Johannessen, and Bernard P. Ricca, *Supporting Beginning English Teachers: Research and Implications for Teacher Induction* (Urbana, Ill.: National Council of Teachers of English, 2005), 55.

2. Ibid.

3. Sonia Nieto, *What Keeps Teachers Going?* (New York and London: Teacher's College Press, 2003), 19. Italics in original.

4. Ibid., 23.

5. McCann et al., *Supporting Beginning English Teachers*, 35.

6. Nieto, *What Keeps Teachers Going?* 77.

How We Came to This Place: Emotional Labor and Stress

Teachers often occupy the role of mother-teacher. This nurturing role often pointed to as a sign of teaching excellence can also be a trait that leads to heightened levels of stress. These teachers, although they most often are women as a result of society-generated gender social roles, can also be men who identify as a nurturer of their students. The term *mother-teacher* does not need to be a gender-specific term. In order to understand why we as teachers are socialized to be nurturers, we need to examine how the history of teaching and the media have led us to this place. I do focus on the female gender in this chapter primarily due to the historical developments that feminized teaching and led to the field of teaching being viewed by society as a type of emotional labor.

Nurturing mother-teachers are teachers who without good, positive coping strategies may experience what I call "nurturance suffering"—emotional labor–induced stress. Most of the researchers I cite in this segment have also focused on women. In the case studies that follow in chapter 3, both male and female teachers are represented.

HISTORICAL PERSPECTIVE

During the course of the nineteenth century, teaching came to be regarded as "women's work" due to the perceived maternal aspects of women, whether present as natural instinct or developed through socialization.[1] At the same

time, child development and well-being came to be regarded as the sole responsibility of the mother. As a result, particular social classes of women were
encouraged to devote their lives to the full-time development of the child
and parental duty. Prior to this change in socialization and expected roles for
women, child rearing was not considered exclusively the work of mothers.[2]

Teaching became the ideal profession for young women and women who
had not yet married, as a way to exercise their nurturing natures and practice
child-rearing skills. In order to limit salaries and encourage women to marry,
an age cap of twenty-eight was enforced and women were no longer allowed
to teach once they had married.[3] Although the female teacher role was initially
designated for when younger children would be in school (summer sessions
and dame schools), increasingly women began to teach during the winter sessions and to teach older students. School boards realized the dual incentive
that not only were women nurturers, but they also could be hired for less.[4]

Several historic reformers also argued for the benefits of women teachers
and teaching as a maternal activity, viewing the school as an extension of the
home. These domestic reformers included Horace Mann, Catherine Beecher,
and John Dewey. Mann argued that not only could women be hired for less
money (women could be hired for half to one-third the wages of men), but
women "could handle the disciplining of the older boys and indeed might do
so better than men because they offered not the discipline of brute force, but
discipline based on their gentle nature.[5] Beecher believed that schools should
be "an appendage of the family state."[6] It was commonly believed that women
were socialized to hold and exhibit different, more nurturing and caring
characteristics than men. It was also believed that by "virtue of their female-
ness, women were thought to be more self-sacrificing and moral than men."[7]
For Dewey, the school was to be womblike and an "embryonic society."[8] Not
only was the female teacher mother to the student but also to an entire new
society born out of the school. Her role was to provide an environment that
would foster such growth and facilitate the metaphorical birth of students as
a new society.

As the feminization of teaching took root, women became the teachers of
the young and men relegated themselves to positions as higher-grade level
teachers and administrators.[9] After Latin was no longer consistently instructed,
teaching was also perceived as less academic and men moved away not only
from teaching the upper grades, but from school teaching altogether, prefer-

ring other careers where they could make more money. Teaching became socially redefined as a female position, in order to prevent a "threat to male virtue."[10] As schools began to request higher levels of training, men also opted out of teaching because for the same level of training they had access to more career options.[11] Teaching became a "pedagogical harem"[12] in which the teachers were female and the administration male as a result of the shift within this now sex-typed employment as men moved away from the classroom.

Yet another reason why women were a popular choice for the teaching field was that women could easily be controlled and "compliance was the key to success."[13] Men were viewed as always looking for advancement, while women it appeared, were content as teachers and were not "scheming for future honors."[14] Complications of the women's role as a teacher included not only an inability for career advancement but also the lack of freedom to express emotion. Those who argued for women as teachers (Horace Mann, Elizabeth Peabody, Catherine Beecher) created what author and educator Madeline Grumet (1988) calls the "cult of maternal nurturance."[15] Grumet explicates the emotional restrictions imposed by this metaphorical cult as women are prohibited, through socialization and cultural expectations, to confess feelings of rage, frustration, or disappointment. These feelings, although potentially manifesting in the female teacher, could not be made public. A further complication and conflict between the historical socialization of women as teachers and the role of schools is that schools require students to move from family intimacy to school anonymity.[16] Parents are typically excluded from the school and teachers are excluded from personal emotional connection to students.

The aspect of cultlike attributes associated with motherhood is a concept that was also highlighted in the work of Ann Douglas (1977). Douglas, in discussing the role of women as mothers in the mid-nineteenth century, points out the emphasis on mother as a "godlike prominence"[17] over her children as these mothers carry out the duties of labor, breast feeding, discipline, and education of the child. Douglas claims that the emphasis on this behavior as the "cult of motherhood . . . was an essential precondition to the flattery American women were trained to demand in place of justice and quality."[18] The acceptance of this perception allowed women a basis for self-respect, a level of prestige, and authority with no real power. Much like Grumet's concept of the "cult of maternal nurturance" these social standards evolved as a means to control women.

Walkerdine (1990) would support this analysis as each social standard was a means of allowing women to feel as if they have value in the system in which they participate, while actually allowing them no power, control, or equality. In Walkerdine's analysis, women are encouraged to think of themselves as nurturers and a balance to the difficulties faced in the world by children, a notable duty. However, this is misleading as women are not allowed the power to change any of these situations; it is an innocuous role simply to placate women into feeling valid. In her text *Schoolgirl Fictions* Walkerdine explores the societal shaping of young girls as "nice, kind and helpful . . . like the teacher."[19] These girls emulate the teachers, continuing the cycle and promoting the "illusion of choice" in the capacity for nurturance.[20]

SOCIALIZATION OF WOMAN AS NURTURER

The socialization of women as nurturers continues in American contemporary culture. Gilligan (1994) notes that in any society the early social environment differs for male and female children. As a result, the personalities of male and female individuals differ. The female identity formation is more likely to incorporate elements of empathy than that of boys. Gilligan cites Chodorow as stating that "girls emerge with a stronger basis for experiencing another's needs and feelings as one's own."[21] As a result women come to judge themselves within a context of human relationships and the ability to care.[22] Individuals are born with a sexual delineation (male or female) but are not born with a specified gender role such as mother. Individuals become mother figures as a result of "historical and social circumstance;"[23] Simone de Beauvoir addresses this belief when stating that "one is not born woman, one becomes woman."[24]

Chodorow (1978) rejects the two basic premises of how women become nurturers. The two most common arguments are biological determinism and social construction. Rather than support either of these arguments, Chodorow instead argues that girls become nurturing mothers as a result of their own interactions with their mother and bases her argument on psychoanalysis and the work of Freud. She believes that the "most important feature of early infantile developments is that this developments occurs *in relation to* another person or persons."[25] Mothers in this argument identify most with their daughters because they are the same gender and do not see them as separate from themselves as they do boys. This primary identification between mothers and daughters leads the daughters to adopt behavior modeled for them by their mothers. It is also "the *wants and needs* which lead women to become mothers [that] put them in situations where their mothering *capacities* can be expressed,"[26] such as in teaching.

Although I do support the belief that in many cases daughters may adopt their mothering and nurturing behaviors from their own mothers, there are many faults in this argument. The first fault that I find with the argument is with the use of Freud's work as rationale. His theories of pseudo-castration, Oedipal stages, and gender identification assert that it is a male gender that is the standard against which women be judged. Chodorow does admit Freud's limitations in that he describes women and female development only in context of a "patriarchal society" and states that he makes "unsupported assertions."[27] Although she questions these aspects of psychoanalytic theory, she continues to use this as a basis for the argument that mothers develop as a result of their relationships with their own mothers.

Chodorow's argument is also based on the construction of a two gender, two member parental unit for the child. She only briefly addresses the challenge to this familial construction by stating that the mothering relationship is a result of the individual providing primary care, in this case the mother need not be the biological mother but may also be a nanny, nurse, or other caregiver. She also briefly addresses the lesbian parental family and uses it as support again by stating that this relationship also re-creates the mother-daughter connection that leads to the development of a desire to mother for the daughter later in life.

The work is effective primarily within the constructs of the traditional family. Single parent families in which a man is the caregiver are not acknowledged, as well as other situations such as foster care, group homes, and homes in which two men together mother the children. Women do not typically stay at home for the entire child-rearing years and this also challenges her construction of a family that identifies its social class by the position of the male power holder or father. Chodorow does acknowledge a changing societal expectation regarding women in the workforce but argues that "nevertheless, family organization and ideology still produce these gender differences and generate expectations that women much more than men will find a primary identity in the family."[28]

Chodorow argues for more involvement of men in childcare believing that this would begin a transformation of the gender-based roles in society and

changes within the division between men and women. Within such a transformation, men would begin to mother and take on nurturing behaviors, in
essence creating equality within the sexual division of labor. She notes that
such a change would "depend on the conscious organization and activity of
all women and men who recognize that their interests lie in transforming the
social organization of gender and eliminating sex inequality."[29]

While the call for greater involvement of men in all nurturing work including parenting and teaching is consistent with the aims of my own research,
others disagree with her approach. Weedon (1987) believes Chodorow's goal
is "over-optimistic because it is necessarily reductionist."[30] Chodorow does
not concern herself with gender politics as a whole, but only those characteristics that connect to the role of mothering. Weedon also criticizes Chodorow
because her argument is based on the "fixed psycho-sexual structures which
look at a single cause."[31] I do agree that the application of Freudian theory
is limiting, but the focus on just one aspect of gender is not as negative as
Weedon implies. By changing just one difference, the doors to changing
others may become available. If one were to focus on all gender inequalities
at once, very little may be accomplished. As Chodorow states, "The social
organization of parenting produces sexual inequality, not simply role differ-
entiation. It is politically and socially important to confront the organization
of parenting."[32] The role of parenting differences and the basic structure of
the parenting system is one basis of many other gender inequalities that exist,
including the lack of nurturing male role models in public institutions like
schools, an issue critical to my own research.

Author and researcher Valerie Walkerdine has also examined the role of
women in teaching and the socialization that distinguishes this specific career
from other aspects of a woman's life. In her article "Progressive Pedagogy
and Political Struggle" Walkerdine (1992) quotes the Hardow Report as taking the position that women were to be educated in order to "amplify their
capacities for maternal nurturance."[33] She goes on to state that it was believed
this aspect of the woman's socialized identity could be enhanced in order
to "provide a quasi-maternal nurturance."[34] Female teachers were expected
to take on a motherlike role for the students, especially in the classrooms of
younger students. It was commonly believed that this attitude would foster
growth in children. Walkerdine asserts the belief that a woman positioned in
this way as a teacher actually played the role of "servant to the omnipotent

child."[35] Women, according to Walkerdine, act as a container to soak up and hold irrationality and often acts of violence that were products of the child's internalization of the culture's patterns of oppression. This absorbing of socially induced child suffering adds to the overall level of stress for the teacher. In her critique of schools, Walkerdine criticizes this expectation that women are to be nurturing.

The role of women as nurturers and the negative effects of such socialized behavior emerge as a focus of consideration in Walkerdine's article. Walkerdine examines the socialized behaviors of women in education, identifying the social belief that the "benevolent gaze of the teacher will secure freedom from cruel authority."[36] While Walkerdine does explicate the nurturing behaviors that women in education are expected to portray, she spends little time on the aspect of acting as "container" for the acting out of student injustice. After briefly mentioning this negative aspect of nurturance, she does not continue her debate by discussing the negative aspects this may have for the teacher. This comes as a surprise for me as a reader considering that she opens the article with the image of herself "sobbing quietly at (her) desk" after a day of frustration. I would have expected a turn toward consideration of her own well-being.

For Walkerdine, it is essential that the issues of nurturing and gender be considered within a political framework, as she believes that it is "important to reassert the centrality of oppression and its transformation into a pathology in terms of a political analysis of the present social order."[37] Walkerdine believes that progressive education fosters powerlessness for the teacher forced to nurture and believes that the classroom is a "site of struggle"[38] in which change can be possible. She does not restrict change to the classroom setting however, believing that the concept of power as connected to the radical bourgeois structure demands that the "formation of the modern state and the modern concept of democratic government"[39] must also be addressed. For Walkerdine, the struggle must go beyond the classroom doors and it is modern politics that must be questioned and transformed.

Although my research is supportive of a commitment to systemic change, the building of a revolutionary movement, which is essentially what Walkerdine advocates, cannot be assigned to teachers as their primary responsibility. It is more effective to encourage the work of nurturing in the classroom in an effort to meet the needs of the students at that moment in time. Walkerdine who sees the role of nurturing as a negative would not agree, instead arguing that it is this nurturing behavior that continues to reinforce an already flawed system.

It is valid to believe that the larger system does need to be addressed, but teachers must also continue to do the daily work of caring for children and teaching content. In order to continue to do this challenging and important work, each teacher must hold on to the conviction that the work is worthwhile and beneficial to the students. All students need nurturing in the context of day-to-day classroom life, but individual students who come from low income or perhaps minority backgrounds and those included in an alternative school setting because they have not succeeded in a typical educational setting need additional nurturing from teachers. This additional nurturing can mitigate the damage inflicted by a system that does not meet the needs of these students and within which they may not feel comfortable or included.

Teacher nurturing may also compensate to some degree for the lack of parental/familial nurturing in some families battling the stresses of surviving on minimum wage salaries in a racist and classist society. Without the guidance of nurturing teachers, these students find themselves vulnerable and manipulated by the larger social and political system that does not value them. It is here that I most disagree with Walkerdine, who would see this nurturing as ineffective for both teacher and student. While the nurturing may be a temporary measure, it is at least one step that teachers can take within their own classrooms to resist the larger structures that impede the work of the school.

By helping disenfranchised students remain within the educational system long enough to develop the tools to fight back against an oppressive society, nurturing teachers are resisting the larger social structure. Students become empowered through awareness and are better armed to advocate for themselves if provided an education that allows them the potential for change. Education as just a series of content lessons will not provide this opportunity. Only when students are provided a nurturing and critical education are they able to achieve this possibility of advocating for themselves in the future.

Whereas Walkerdine spends more time examining why negative behavior by students enters into the classroom and the role of women in creating "civilized children" through "quasi-maternal nurturance"[40] in progressive education, I choose to focus more on the teacher and the implications of nurturing behavior on one's own well-being. There should not be a "denial of pain, of oppression"[41] for children or for the teachers who nurture them. This pain needs to be examined in terms of every player on the stage, student and teacher alike. Much has been made of the social world of children and the oppressions they experience every day; now I argue the same be afforded to teachers. The social image of teacher as impervious to pain inflicted by students (directly or indirectly) must be shattered. Despite the portrayal of teachers as saints in popular film and novels, they too experience both emotional pain and political oppression.

The contradictions in expected behavior by teachers and the reality of the work must also be examined. The social images of teachers create a level of expectation that is internalized by the teacher, an expectation that one may not be able to execute given the constraints of human nature. Teaching as an emotional labor, unlike many other professions, cannot be left at the workplace.

I picked up where Walkerdine leaves off discussing nurturance by expanding on her term through my concept of *nurturance suffering* (the stress and emotional responses that result from nurturing behavior by the teacher in the school setting). This concept appears in several of the case studies of chapter 3.

All too aware of the social contradictions that enter the classroom, teachers absorb student pain as Walkerdine (1992) posits, "Woman as container soaks up and contains the irrationality which she best understands."[42] This pain once absorbed, however, does not simply disappear. I argue that it collects as nurturance suffering, manifesting as both emotional and physical stress that the teacher carries with her from the classroom. Anger, worry, sadness, and fear are not left in the classroom with the week's test exams to be graded or addressed the following Monday. These emotions are carried home to interfere with the teacher's life outside of school. Without coping mechanisms, this nurturance-related stress could build up, creating negative consequences for the teacher.

The socialized expectations for female emotional behavior extend beyond the teaching profession. In her text *The Managed Heart* researcher Arlie Russell Hochschild (2003)[43] examines the commercialization of human emotion in such public service careers as flight attendants. This "emotional labor" requires an individual to overcome one's personal emotional connections and instead put on that smiling face to deliver the expected emotional goods. This labor expectation of flight attendants and other public service employees has many parallels to the criticisms Walkerdine makes of the emotional expectations of teachers. Regardless of treatment by the customer, emotional laborers are expected to smile and progress through the labor. This management of feeling creates a cost for the worker in that she may "become estranged or alienated from an aspect of self—either the body or the margins of the soul—that is used to do the work."[44] Thus, the teacher who is overwhelmed by the emotional investment required to put on a happy face may shut down that part of her emotional being that responds to students in a genuine manner. This emotional distancing was documented by Hochschild in her work with flight attendants who in the process of their work became damaged emotionally. According to Hochschild, it is women who are most vulnerable to this difficulty because "of all *women* working, roughly one-half have jobs that call for emotional labor."[45]

Stress resulting from emotional labor can be found in the teaching profession. The emotional laborer must manage the "estrangement between self and feeling and between self and display."[46] Unfortunately, for many women in careers of emotional labor, it is the managing of feeling that is perceived to be the problem when women react negatively to this stress. The causes of the anger or other emotional reactions are not acknowledged as the catalyst of the performance problem, nor are the overall work conditions. These work issues are "treated as unalterable facts of life."[47] The problem from the perspective of the employer (and male-dominated culture) becomes how this woman can better control her emotional responses and not let the interactions with her customers affect her performance. Inappropriate behaviors from the public served are considered acceptable, and it must be the worker who manages emotion to serve an ungrateful public.

The work that Hochschild characterizes as emotional labor shares three qualities with teaching: it requires face-to-face or voice-to-voice communication with the public; it requires the worker to produce an emotional state in another person; and third, it allows the employer to exercise control over the emotional activities of employees.[48] Teachers are face-to-face with students on a daily basis and for extended periods of time. Unlike in a flight attendant's situation, when once the flight is over the individuals may never have contact again, a teacher continues class after class to interact with the students, sometimes for more than one school year. Teachers' emotional well-being may be challenged when dealing not only with disruptive students or students who present behavior problems in class, but also with students who cannot be nurtured and protected beyond the classroom door. Teachers are expected by administration and the public to project a demeanor of caring and to control their emotions when interacting with students. Although, to an extent, both genders are expected to display similar emotional behaviors, women have different socialized expectations. The teaching profession holds one set of behavior expectations for women and another for men. For instance, according to Hochschild, when a man expresses anger,

> it is deemed "rational" or understandable anger, anger that indicates not weakness of character but deeply held conviction. When women express an equivalent degree of anger, it is more likely to be interpreted as a sign of personal instability. It is believed women are more emotional, and this very belief is used to invalidate their feelings. That is, the women's feelings are seen not as a response to real events but as reflections of themselves as "emotional" women.[49]

There is a conflict in emotional states between what a woman's socialization expects and the expectations placed by a historically male administration when paired with the social understanding of distance between students and teachers. This creates a discord for the female teacher who has been socialized to be a nurturing quasi-mother, yet must remain distanced from emotional investment in her students.

Although buildings and districts with only male administrations are no longer the norm, the legacy of this dichotomy remains as many female administrators continue the status quo. Rockhill, in her work with critical literacy, points to this behavior as women being "trained like a rat to run through and perform effectively" in the maze created by men.[50] Rather than climb the walls created by male administrations in the past and forge new roads independently, many women choose to run the established maze. By continuing to take the established path, they deepen the grooves in the maze, making it harder for those in the future who may choose to climb the wall instead.

MEN MOTHER-TEACHER TOO

Alan Johnson (2001), author of *Privilege, Power and Difference*,[51] includes an examination of the role men play specifically in this issue of gender in teaching. In his text, Johnson examines the roles of those individuals who are subjugated in our society and offers some potential methods that if applied to the topic of nurturance suffering may create a "revisioning" of the issue. Johnson notes that the perception of women as more nurturing carries over into the college atmosphere as well and that "students hold their female college professors . . . to a much higher standard of caring and emotional availability than they do male teachers."[52] According to Johnson, this creates a "double bind that is one of the hallmarks of social oppression."[53] In this case, the woman can be devalued no matter what the circumstances. If she is too caring, her credibility is questioned and she is unable to be successful in the male model; yet if she denies this nurturing aspect of self, she is considered less than woman.

For Johnson, this double bind is exacerbated by a sense of individualistic thinking, which pervades our society. It is this thinking that makes discussing these issues a problem and "encourages women to . . . blame and distrust men."[54] When issues of this nature are brought up, men are left to feel personally attacked and defensively label the situation "as a 'women's problem.'"[55] Thus, the issue is devalued and becomes something of a stereotyped stigma associated with women similar to those of emotional outbursts and hot flashes. Men are able to excuse themselves from culpability and instead blame whom they identify as "sexist men." Johnson points out that this creates a kind of "paralysis: people either talk about sexism in the most superficial, unthreatening, trivializing and stupid ways, or they don't talk about it at all."[56]

The issue of gender stereotype is also reinforced through what Johnson calls a "culture of denial."[57] Those of privilege ignore what does not directly confront them, and it is easier to pretend an issue does not exist rather than to acknowledge it and attempt resolution. Johnson also notes that those in power become offended when issues such as these are brought to the surface and that they are annoyed when the issues enter discussion. Those in power often respond with simple reactions such as downplaying the severity of the issue.

Walkerdine notes similar arguments to those of Johnson when explaining the "illusion of choice."[58] Here it is not just denial that reinforces the problem, but the further complication that women are led to believe they have a choice and control over their own role as a nurturer. Women in this framework are colluding with those in power by allowing such an illusion to exist. By accepting societal stereotypes through false negotiation in the belief they can choose whether to participate in that image, women allow the stereotype to grow and only reinforce the power of the elite by ignoring the root issue. There is no real choice in the matter, as to deny the stereotype that women are nurturers only heightens the belief that this woman then is in denial of her femininity and is "acting male." For women, teaching is seen as an extension of their role within the family structure. Women are nurturers and men provide leadership. Margaret Adams calls this "the compassion trap."[59] Despite all the contradictions, women continue to fulfill the same roles asked of them in the early 1900s. This maintains the status quo even under the guise of choice. Women take on the position of "transmitters of cultural norms rather than cultural transformers"[60] because they are still operating within a framework designed by men to maintain male dominance and power.

For Johnson, the belief that women are trapped in the contradiction and with the illusion of choice is a result of individuals following the "path of least resistance."[61] Both genders contribute to the problem because it is so much easier to ignore the issue and assume that if an individual really wanted to, she or he could break free. Johnson also notes that many people follow this path because it is the only one they see. Because of how individuals are positioned in society, they see no other opportunities to break away from the norm, and in fact, would not even recognize that the norm has flaws. The individual comfortable in the association with the dominate culture has no desire to break away from the social norm as it reinforces and maintains the position of power.

In order to break away from the social norm and effect change, some theorists insist on a holistic perspective that acknowledges how both genders participate in the cultivation of such bias.[62] Walkerdine opposes this idea and instead calls for a "new reading [that will] permit the possibility of struggle to work for transformation."[63] She encourages a splintering and deconstruction approach to address the issue of gender bias in order to allow for exploration of other possibilities. This breaking away of genders from each other and examination of particular roles each plays may lead to a blame game in which no ground is gained in order to solve the issue at hand. This aspect also separates gender issues from each other rather than examines how they reinforce each other.

Because I, like Johnson, believe in the "matrix of domination"[64] in which every form of privilege is part of a large system, I do not believe a splintering is the best approach. This leads too easily to further creation of denial barriers to protect one's dominant status. In addition, I do not feel that nurturing behavior is something that should be removed from one's development as a woman but instead feel that this should be added to the conception and development of male as a gender. A solution can only be reached if there is participation by both genders in society and active decisions to participate on a different level to restructure the existing system of gender definition. The entire system must be called into question and people must become aware of how their "behaviors limit their effectiveness"[65] to contribute to change. Rather than splinter the genders in disagreement, a wholeness must be obtained and a total "revisioning" must occur.

> For "woman," well imprinted with the sociocultural heritage, has been inculcated with the spirit of "restraint." She is in fact "restraint" itself, socially. She restrains herself, and is restrained, by a thousand bonds, hitched, conjugated, strings, chains, nets, leashes, feeding dish, network of servile, reassuring dependencies. . . . They have taught you to be afraid of the abyss, of the infinite, which is nonetheless more familiar to you than it is to men. Don't go near the abyss! If she should discover its (her) force! If she should, suddenly, take pleasure in, profit from its immensity! If she should take the leap! And fall not like a stone, but like a bird. If she should discover herself to be a swimmer of the unlimited![66]

As Cixous suggests, there is power in recognizing the strength of one's position. A nurturing woman does have power and strength, but because nurturing has been marginalized rather than celebrated, it is seen as a weakness. Nurturing women are not victims of their position, instead they are champions. The nurturing teacher is willing to emotionally connect with students despite the risks and she should be empowered by her actions. I propose that not only do women need to jump the abyss and realize this power, but women need to take hand with men and bring them along, allowing men to participate in nurturing behavior. In order to do this, first we must find the road to that abyss and imagine what is on the other side. Peter McLaren would suggest that in order to do this, society must be willing to participate in discovering the "arch of social dreaming."[67] This poetic imagery refers to the act of revisioning what exists in society so that the arch connecting this reality and the utopian social dream can be constructed.

Rachel Naomi Remen (1999) addresses the belief that compassion and nurturing must be brought into the schools. In her article "Educating for Mission, Meaning and Compassion," Remen states that "recovering compassion requires us to confront the shadow of our culture directly."[68] Our culture values what she calls the "values of the frontier," those values that heighten isolation and self-sufficiency. It is these values that prevent our society from joining hands and approaching an abyss together. Too much emphasis has been placed on the ability of the individual to function in isolation and reject the help of others.

Nurturing behavior is not something that should be eliminated from schools; instead it could be encouraged for both genders. Men must join in the act of nurturing and recognize the "impoverishment to their emotional and spiritual lives, the price they pay in personal authenticity and integrity, how they compromise their humanity, how they limit the connections they can have with other people."[69] By joining together in a common mission, the "arch of social dreaming" can be achieved and changes can begin.

WHY TEACHERS ARE EXPECTED TO CARE: MOTHER-TEACHER AND THE IMPACT OF THE MEDIA

Through the media, specific images of women as teachers have prevailed over time. In literature, television, and film, female teachers are consistently portrayed as saintly mother figures, who are capable of saving even the most difficult of students. This building of stereotype continually shapes the next generation of teachers. It is the "hero teacher"[70] portrayed in the media that young people entering the field of education emulate and that creates a bank of stereotypes that must be consistently battled. The stereotypes found in popular culture enter into the play of children and "play a formative role in the evolution of a teacher's identity, and are part of the enculturation of teachers into their professions."[71] New teachers draw upon their past experiences and the presentations of teaching in the media as they begin to shape their own teaching identities. When these presentations of teacher image fail the new teacher, the teacher must make adjustments to balance socialized expectations and the reality of the situation. As Weber and Mitchell (1995) point out, "Teacher identity can be seen as a tension between the expected/desired and the experienced."[72] It is "television and other forms of popular culture [that] serve as the first school for young children and as the first Faculty of Education for adults who wish to become teachers."[73]

Films such as *Music of the Heart*[74] and *Dangerous Minds*[75] both present middle-aged white women who enter teaching later in life as a last resort and take positions teaching in urban schools. In both films, the teachers are able to find success in *saving* the urban Black/Hispanic youth by using nontraditional teaching methods and displaying nurturing behavior toward the students. Films such as these present a false sense of what teaching is, and the audience absorbs these messages in the transaction of viewing the work. The films both display a belief that "schools and teachers are in the business of saving children [and that] most teachers are simply not up to the challenge."[76]

Other popular images of teachers come from television media such as shows like *The Simpsons, Saved by the Bell*, and *Boston Public*.[77] These shows, which target younger audiences, continue to portray female teachers with a host of stereotypes. The satirical show *The Simpsons* portrays teachers as "objects of ridicule" and as "lazy, uninspired, authoritarian, pessimistic and incompetent."[78] These teachers are not successful as they work with the primary character Bart Simpson. Bart's teacher, Edna Krabappel, is portrayed as a stressed out, chain-smoking, divorced, middle-aged women, although the show does portray her as having heart and develops her beyond the flat character one typically encounters in a cartoon format. Often, the creators of the show allow the audience a view of Edna's personal life outside of school, but she primarily "reflects a stereotypical image of the historical spinster teacher."[79]

The teachers from the now-cancelled show *Saved by the Bell* also operate from a basis of stereotypes as do the students portrayed in the show. Teachers are, as in the show *The Simpsons*, supporting characters. Here the main female teacher, Miss Bliss, again is a single woman, but in contrast to Edna Krabappel, Miss Bliss is attractive and sympathetic to the student's needs. She is portrayed as a nurturing female teacher who becomes close to several of the students, interacting with them on a personal level as they navigate teenage high school drama. While Edna is an elementary school teacher who cannot function without her teacher copy of the text because it has all the answers, Miss Bliss teaches high school English and is creative in her classroom. She reinforces the stereotype of teacher as saint and mother.

Boston Public, the Fox television show that had a short lifetime, takes a much different approach to portraying teachers. While *The Simpsons* and

Saved by the Bell are both comedies, this show is identified as drama and realistic. The series explores the personal and professional lives of teachers and administrators working at a midsize high school in Boston. The female teachers on this show are all attractive young women who teach with passion and are ready to challenge those who contradict their nontraditional methods. There are three primary female characters as teachers. Two of the characters are young (in their twenties) and are slim, very attractive women. The third character is a heavyset woman in her early thirties. The show tends to focus much of the airtime exploring the personal lives of the teachers and portrays the two slim women as sex objects. Conversations in the teacher lounge often center around sex talk and include all of the teachers on some level. The portrayal of women in this show is mixed, as on one level they all care very deeply for the students and their instruction, but at the same time they are displayed as having loose morals and a propensity for attracting controversy.

Literature much like visual media also communicates stereotype and continues to promote specific images of women as nurturing teachers. The young adult novel *Staying Fat for Sarah Byrnes* by Chris Crutcher (1993)[80] displays one female teacher who takes the nurturing aspect to an extreme level. In this novel, a young girl named Sarah was burned across most of her face as a child and later in the novel the reader learns that her burns were the result of abuse by her father. The female teacher, Ms. Lemry, teaches a course called Contemporary American Thought in which the main character Eric and his best friend Sarah are enrolled. The course becomes very controversial and is questioned by the administration and the students stand up in defense of the teacher. At the same time, the primary plot of Eric helping Sarah come to terms with her abuse enters a place in which he must seek adult assistance and he turns to Ms. Lemry. Eric becomes close to this teacher because she is also his swim coach and Eric arrives at her house to explain his problem.

This teacher displays qualities of nurturing while she helps both Eric and Sarah through this difficult time in their personal lives; however, she goes much farther than the classroom and takes young Sarah to Reno to find her mother. Later she hides Sarah in her house so that her father can't find her, and by the conclusion of the text adopts Sarah. Ms. Lemry takes the aspect of female teacher as nurturer to an extreme. She does not represent a metaphorical mothering in the classroom, but takes the role of actual mother to the character abandoned by her biological mother. She also displays other stereotypical images of teacher behavior as outlined in Joseph and Burnaford's text (2001),[81] such as teacher as saint and savior who reaches students through nontraditional means.

Young people reading this novel may view this teacher as a hero, whose intervention saved the character of Sarah. In reality, this behavior would not be tolerated in a school district and the portrayal of this teacher provides a template for teaching that is not representative of the reality of teaching. It is these portrayals of female teachers that consistently reinforce false notions of what a female teacher is in the actual school setting.

Even Barbie has participated in the generation and perpetuation of female teacher stereotypes. Weber and Mitchell (1995)[82] analyze a Marvel comic in which Barbie takes on the role of a student teacher assigned to teach art history. As the story plays out, Barbie doubts her own ability to teach until she finds value in caring and nurturing a young female student. At the close of the comic, "Barbie reveals her true love of teaching and implicitly positions woman-as-teacher in the role of selfless and devoted nurturer."[83] The favorable images of female teachers include traits such as "self-sacrificing, kind, overworked, underpaid and [as] holding an unlimited reservoir of patience."[84]

The images presented in popular culture create a socialized expectation of what it means to be a female teacher. Even when these stereotypes are in conflict with each other, such as the chain-smoking Ms. Krabappel and the sexualized yet virginal Barbie, each still displays nurturing traits. Because of these images, women begin to validate themselves based on the ability to nurture. As young children caring for a doll or playing at teacher, the acceptance of these images is internalized to later manifest in the way female teachers approach the classroom. In some cases, the female teacher is able to reposition the self after the disillusionment of teaching, and in others, the female teacher still adheres to this image and alters her world view around the concept in order to allow room for the view of female teacher as nurturer to still function.

The socialized view of female teachers as nurturers has had a long history with the support of many prominent educational voices. This trend continues today and is reinforced through popular media. The role that women are led to play does not come without a cost as Walkerdine and Hochschild point out. Stress and in the extreme case, burnout are potential hazards of emotional labor.

TEACHER STRESS: BEYOND EMOTIONAL LABOR

Other factors that must be considered in the potential for developing nurturance-related stress connect to the manner in which schools are constructed and operate. When a threatening or potentially threatening event occurs, an individual must weigh the perceived demands and judge the demand against his or her ability to cope or meet the demand.[85]

Stress "can be considered any factor, acting internally or externally, that makes it difficult to adapt and that induces increased effort on the person to maintain a state of equilibrium."[86] According to McCarthy and Wood, "Teacher stress may be seen as the perception of an imbalance between the demands at the school and the resources teachers have for coping."[87] When this lack of ability to cope reaches a peak, teachers experience an extreme form of stress known as burnout. Burnout is described as "a loss of idealism and enthusiasm for work."[88] This is different than the typical stressors encountered in teaching, which one can overcome through coping mechanisms.

Individuals have many reactions to stress, which may be placed on a sliding scale between positive and beneficial reactions that help solve the problem and those responses that are debilitating to the individual. Responses typically fall into two categories: those that are physiological and those that are behavioral.[89] While many of the responses are a temporary development with no long-lasting effect, such as a rapid beating of the heart or perspiration, nurturance suffering has a long-lasting effect due to the combination of both physiological and behavioral aspects. Also, unlike an increase in perspiration, nurturance suffering will return, triggered by the same precipitating issue as the mind consistently revisits that issue and allows it to interfere with other activities. The precipitating issues for nurturance suffering are not as easily solved as a misplaced file, for instance, as they are directly linked to human emotions and the well-being of students. As this stress is allowed to build up, the individual may be at risk for burnout.

In the 1980s two researchers, Christina Maslach and Susan Jackson,[90] reexamined the term *burnout* and developed several subdomains of the general term. They included in these groupings: (1) depersonalization in which the individual separates self from others and begins to view others impersonally, (2) reduced personal accomplishment in which the individual begins to devalue the work of self and others, and (3) emotional exhaustion in which the individual begins to feel a lack of emotional resilience and is highly vulnerable to even the less significant stressors.[91] Teachers may be at an even greater risk of experiencing stress due to the depersonalization and sense of isolation that is often experienced by teachers throughout the school day.[92]

The sense of isolation from peers is an aspect that DeMarrais and LeCompte (1999)[93] discuss in their text when addressing the role of stress. The motel-like configuration of classrooms, combined with the scheduling constraints of the work day, enhance the sense of isolation experienced by teachers. Teachers tend to spend most of the school day in their own classrooms without peer interaction. This sense of disconnectedness strengthens the risk for burnout as teachers cannot decompress the accumulated stressors of the day.

Once teachers begin to experience stress accumulation or are on the verge of burnout, they may experience several upsetting emotions. These emotions may include a perception that the work is futile and that the work is inconsistent with ideals, resulting in a conception of role conflict.[94] Symptoms may include feelings of alienation and isolation (with a focus on meaninglessness), powerlessness, and both physical and mental exhaustion. DeMarrais and LeCompte explain that these feelings may be exacerbated and stress may develop when "rewards do not seem commensurate with the effort expended."[95] Alienation, for these authors, includes the sense that "life has become meaningless and that one is powerless to make the changes necessary to restore meaning to one's life and work."[96]

Humphrey (1992) attributes the increased stress level of teachers to several factors including the high level of decision making in a day, public scrutiny, schools as a high risk area for violence, and the need for a high level of sensitivity in responding to each student.[97] He also notes that teachers are highly ineffectual in coping with stress. As a result of a study of surveys among teachers regarding stress, Humphrey found that "49% of respondents indicated that they are more or less at a loss on how to deal with stress"[98] and had no strategies other than to simply tolerate the stress.

A study completed by Geoff Troman and Peter Wood (2002)[99] on teacher burnout placed teachers into three general resultant categories when reacting to stress and burnout. At the extreme end of the continuum, teachers end their careers as professional educators. The second category included teachers who "downshift" by redefining their roles in the school and taking on less demanding responsibilities. The third reaction to stress as defined by this study included those teachers who choose to remain teaching in the same capacity, but build up their out of school interests in an effort to find balance. Yet another reaction in an effort to find stability is the teacher who emotionally removes the self as a form of coping, as is described by the work of Maslach and Jackson.

Hochschild (2003) also discusses the reactions to emotional labor with parallels to the emotional responses cited above. The first response she describes is shown by the individual who responds through depersonalization, which makes the individual more likely to suffer stress and burnout. The individual will become passive, remote, and detached from the people who are served through the work. The second response is emotional numbness, creating an emotional shell to keep from responding with genuine emotion. A third response is seen in the individual who creates what Hochschild refers to as a "healthy estrangement" in which the individual clearly separates self from role, defining different acting responses to work and to a personal life outside of work.[100] Although in the final case, the individual is less likely to experience burnout, it may be argued that this "acting" may result in career dissatisfaction and an inability to be genuine with other individuals at work. Women are at a greater danger of "overdeveloping this false self and losing track of its boundaries"[101] due to the socialized nurturing role for women.

A research study based on survey responses in Western Australia in 1984 indicated that gender differences were related to the expressions of stress for teachers in the field of education. This study, conducted through survey questionnaires, examined teacher stress and the factors that may influence the development of stress, including salary differences, lack of promotion possibilities, and limited rewards of teaching and success with students.[102]

Although aspects such as salary were identified as important by both genders, women were much more likely than men to consider recognition from administration as important to job satisfaction. The study also found that among only the female teachers was there a "significant correlation with distress when they felt unable to be on close terms with the students" and when students were distressed and did not seek out the teacher for assistance.[103] One of the findings of this study was the "disparate values placed by male and female teachers upon intrinsic and extrinsic rewards and satisfaction of teaching." Another finding was that the "occurrence of psychological distress among secondary teachers is twice that expected in the general population" as measured by the General Health Questionnaire

(GHQ), which was developed to measure psychological stress, both through physical and mental symptoms.[104]

In terms of nurturing behavior exhibited by teachers, society leads us to believe that it is women who do this work. In reality, both men and women partake in emotional labor and experience stress as a result. The case studies in chapter 3 include examples of both men and women who display nurturing behaviors toward students and suffer as a result. It should also be remembered that other stress factors will impact the individual as well and that nurturance sufferance does not typically manifest in isolation of other stressful factors.

NOTES

1. Madeleine R. Grumet, *Bitter Milk: Women and Teaching* (Amherst: University of Massachusetts Press, 1988); Pamela Bolotin Joseph and Gail E. Burnaford, eds., *Images of Schoolteachers in America*, 2nd ed. (Mahwah, N.J.: Lawrence Erlbaum Associates, 2001); Joel Perlmann and Robert A. Margo, *Women's Work: American School Teachers, 1650–1920* (Chicago: University of Chicago Press, 2001); Redding S. Sugg, Jr., *Motherteacher: The Feminization of American Education* (Charlottesville: University Press of Virginia, 1978).

2. Maxine Margolis, *Mothers and Such: Views of American Women and Why They Changed* (Berkeley: University of California Press, 1984), 12.

3. Redding S. Sugg, Jr., *Motherteacher: The Feminization of American Education* (Charlottesville: University Press of Virginia, 1978), 126.

4. Joel Perlmann and Robert A. Margo, *Women's Work: American School Teachers, 1650–1920* (Chicago: University of Chicago Press, 2001).

5. Ibid., 29.

6. Sugg, *Motherteacher: The Feminization of American Education*, 50.

7. Ibid., 48.

8. Ibid., 184.

9. Madeleine R. Grumet, *Bitter Milk: Women and Teaching* (Amherst: University of Massachusetts Press, 1988), 25.

10. Sugg, *Motherteacher: The Feminization of American Education*, 3.

11. Grumet, *Bitter Milk: Women and Teaching*, 36–37; Perlmann and Margo, *Women's Work: American School Teachers*, 101.

12. Kathleen DeMarrais and Margaret LeCompte, *The Way Schools Work: A Sociological Analysis of Education*, 3rd ed. (New York: Addison Wesley Longman, 1999), 70.

13. Grumet, *Bitter Milk: Women and Teaching*, 36–37; Perlmann and Margo, *Women's Work: American School Teachers*, 43.

14. Ibid.

15. Grumet, *Bitter Milk: Women and Teaching*, 52.

16. Ibid., 170.

17. Ann Douglas, *The Feminization of American Culture* (New York: Alfred A. Knopf, Inc., 1977), 75.

18. Ibid.

19. Valerie Walkerdine, *Schoolgirl Fictions* (London and New York: Verso, 1990), 76.

20. Ibid., 54.

21. Nancy Chodorow, *The Reproduction of Mothering: Psychoanalysis and the Sociology of Gender* (Berkeley: University of California Press, 1978), 28.

22. Carol Gilligan, "Women's Place in a Man's Life Cycle," in *The Education Feminism Reader*, ed. Lynda Stone (New York and London: Routledge, 1994), 35.

23. Sara Ruddick, *Maternal Thinking: Toward a Politics of Peace* (Boston: Beacon Press, 1995), 52.

24. Quoted in Verena Andermatt Conley, *Hélène Cixous: Writing the Feminine* (Lincoln: University of Nebraska Press, 1984), 6.

25. Chodorow, *The Reproduction of Mothering*, 77. Italics in original.

26. Ibid., 205. Italics in original.

27. Ibid., 142.

28. Ibid., 175.

29. Ibid., 61.

30. Chris Weedon, *Feminist Practice and Poststructuralist Theory* (New York: Blackwell Publishers, 1987), 62.

31. Ibid.

32. Chodorow, *The Reproduction of Mothering*, 214.

33. Valerie Walkerdine, "Progressive Pedagogy and Political Struggle," in *Feminisms and Critical Pedagogy*, eds. Carmen Luke and Jennifer Gore (New York: Routledge, 1992), 18.

34. Ibid.

35. Ibid., 21.

36. Ibid., 16.

37. Ibid., 21.

38. Ibid., 22.

39. Ibid., 15.

40. Ibid., 18.

41. Ibid., 20.

42. Ibid., 21.

43. Arlie Hochschild, *The Managed Heart: Commercialization of Human Feeling*. (Berkeley: University of California Press, 2003).

44. Ibid., 7.

45. Ibid., 11. Italics in original.

46. Ibid., 131.

47. Ibid., 113.

48. Ibid., 147.

49. Ibid., 173.

50. Kathleen Rockhill, "Dis/connecting Literacy and Sexuality: Speaking the Unspeakable in the Classroom," in *Critical Literacy: Politics, Praxis and the Postmodern*, eds. Colin Lankshear and Peter L. McLaren (Albany: State University of New York Press, 1993), 352.

51. Alan Johnson, *Privilege, Power and Difference* (New York: McGraw-Hill Higher Education, 2001).

52. Ibid., 106.

53. Ibid.

54. Ibid., 84.

55. Ibid.

56. Ibid., 84–85.

57. Ibid., 69.

58. Walkerdine, *Schoolgirl Fictions*, 54.

59. Margaret Adams as cited in Patti Lather, "The Absent Presence: Patriarchy, Capitalism and the Nature of Teacher Work," in *The Education Feminism Reader*, ed. Lynda Stone (New York and London: Routledge, 1994), 245.

60. Lather, "The Absent Presence," 245.

61. Johnson, *Privilege, Power and Difference*, 87.

62. Steven Glazer, ed., *The Heart of Learning: Spirituality in Education* (New York: Penguin Putnam, 1999), 10.

63. Walkerdine, *Schoolgirl Fictions*, 57.

64. Johnson, *Privilege, Power and Difference*, 54.

65. Ibid., 142.

66. Hélène Cixous, "Coming to Writing" (1991) as cited in Abigail Bray, *Hélène Cixous: Writing and Sexual Difference* (New York: Palgrave Macmillan, 2004), 177.

67. Peter McLaren, "Critical Literacy and the Postmodern Turn," in *Critical Literacy: Politics, Praxis and the Postmodern*, eds. Colin Lankshear and Peter L. McLaren (Albany: State University of New York Press, 1993), 411.

68. Rachel Naomi Remen, "Educating for Mission, Meaning and Compassion," in *The Heart of Learning: Spirituality in Education*, ed. Steven Glazer (New York: Penguin Putnam, 1999), 35.

69. Johnson, *Privilege, Power and Difference*, 169.

70. Pamela Bolotin Joseph and Gail E. Burnaford, eds., *Images of Schoolteachers in America*, 2nd ed. (Mahwah, N.J.: Lawrence Erlbaum Associates, 2001), 173.

71. Sandra Weber and Claudia Mitchell, *That's Funny, You Don't Look Like a Teacher! Interrogating Images and Identity in Popular Culture* (London and Washington, D.C.: Falmer Press, 1995), 27.

72. Ibid., 31.

73. Ibid., 128.

74. Wes Craven, director, and Pamela Gray, writer, *Music of the Heart* [Motion Picture]. (United States: Miramax/Walt Disney Home Video, 1999).

75. John N. Smith, director, and Ronald Bass, screenplay writer, *Dangerous Minds* [Motion Picture]. (United States: Hollywood Pictures, 1995).

76. William Ayers, "A Teacher Ain't Nothin' but a Hero: Teachers and Teaching in Film," in *Images of Schoolteachers in America*, 2nd ed., eds. Pamela Bolotin Joseph and Gail E Burnaford (Mahwah, N.J.: Lawrence Erlbaum Associates, 2001), 201.

77. Matt Groening, creator and executive producer, *The Simpsons* [Television Series]. (FOX, 1989–2009); Marcia Govons and Franco E. Bario, producers, *Saved by the Bell* [Television Series]. (NBC, 1989–1993); David E. Kelly, executive producer, *Boston Public* [Television Series]. (FOX, 2000).

78. Ken Kantor, Nancy Lerner Kantor, Josh Kantor, Mary Eaton, and Benjamin Kantor, "'I Will Not Expose the Ignorance of the Faculty': The Simpsons as School Satire," in *Images of Schoolteachers in America*, 2nd ed., eds. Pamela Bolotin Joseph and Gail E. Burnaford (Mahwah, N.J.: Lawrence Erlbaum Associates, 2001), 186.

79. Ibid., 188.

80. Chris Crutcher, *Staying Fat for Sarah Byrnes* (New York: HarperCollins Children's Books, 1993).

81. Joseph and Burnaford, *Images of Schoolteachers in America.*

82. Weber and Mitchell, *That's Funny, You Don't Look Like a Teacher!*

83. Ibid., 112.

84. Ibid., 113.

85. Chris McCarthy and Terri Wood, "Understanding and Preventing Teacher Burnout," *ERIC Digest*, December 2002, at www.ericsp.org/pages/digests/02-03.pdf (accessed April 25, 2003).

86. James Harry Humphrey, *Stress among Women in Modern Society* (Springfield, Ill.: Charles C. Thomas, 1992), 16.

87. McCarthy and Wood, "Understanding and Preventing Teacher Burnout," 1.

88. Ibid.

89. Humphrey, *Stress among Women in Modern Society*, 21.

90. Maslach and Jackson as cited in McCarthy and Wood, "Understanding and Preventing Teacher Burnout."

91. Ibid.

92. Ibid., 2.

93. Kathleen DeMarrais and Margaret LeCompte, *The Way Schools Work: A Sociological Analysis of Education*, 3rd ed. (New York: Addison Wesley Longman, 1999).

94. McCarthy and Wood, "Understanding and Preventing Teacher Burnout."

95. DeMarrais and LeCompte, *The Way Schools Work*, 170.

96. Ibid.

97. Humphrey, *Stress among Women in Modern Society*, 96.

98. Ibid., 99.

99. Troman and Wood as cited by McCarthy and Wood, "Understanding and Preventing Teacher Burnout," 9.

100. Arlie Hochschild, *The Managed Heart: Commercialization of Human Feeling* (Berkeley: University of California Press, 2003), 187–88.

101. Ibid., 195.

102. Elizabeth Tuettemann, "Teaching: Stress and Satisfaction," *Issues in Educational Research* 1, no. 1 (1991), at www.education.curtin.edu.au/iier/iier1/tuettemann.html (accessed April 25, 2003).

103. Ibid., 10.

104. Ibid., 9.

2

Coping with Nurturance Suffering

(And All the Other Stress That Comes with Being a Great Teacher)

NURTURANCE SUFFERING QUIZ

Determine the impact of caring for students on your own well-being. Answer honestly the questions and prompts below:

1. Do you find that students disclose personal information to you? Either through writing or direct conversation?
2. Do you find that you often worry about your students and events related to their personal lives?
3. Do you think about or worry about your students outside of the school day?
4. Are you unable to leave school at school? Does your work and worry often come home with you?
5. When thinking about students and their problems, do you encounter symptoms of stress?
6. Do you have a sense of powerlessness at school?
7. Do you have a colleague that you can speak with about work and worries?
8. Are you able to sleep easily at night and fall asleep without worry?
9. Do you look forward to your work and seeing students?
10. Are you supported emotionally by your administration?
11. Do you feel as if your administrators and colleagues care about your work with students? Is your work valued by others?

12. Do you find that during the school day you feel anxious or stressed due to interactions with students?
13. Do you smoke, drink, or use other substances to alleviate stress from work?
14. Do you find that you dread attending work?

If you answered yes to questions 1–6 and 12–14 you may be experiencing nurturance suffering due to your work with students. It is important to note that other causes of stress can also factor into your evaluation of your work and that often we do not experience nurturance suffering in isolation. In some cases, we become more susceptible to feelings of nurturance suffering due to other mitigating factors such as conflicts at home and a heavy workload.

If you answered yes to number 13, you are actually putting yourself at risk for even higher rates of stress and stress impacts. Poor coping mechanisms exacerbate feelings of stress and in the long run will only make your situation worse. These poor coping mechanisms should be replaced with more positive strategies such as ones found later in this chapter. By incorporating positive strategies and altering the work environment, you may alleviate your overwhelming feelings of stress while still doing the very important work of caring.

If you answered yes to questions 7–9, the good news is that you do have some support to help cope with the stress of caring. Without these supports, the work becomes much more difficult.

STRESS AND NURTURANCE SUFFERING

The term *stress* became popularized in the early twentieth century in reference to the state of mental health. The root of the term came from the field of engineering and was often coupled with the term *strain* as in a risk to structural damage. Stress was often linked to worry, work, fatigue, and life changing events. Early understandings of stress were viewed as an individual's inability to adjust to life.[1]

Stress is most often seen in a negative light and as an element that will be harmful to the individual. There can, however, be some good forms of stress that help an individual recognize the importance of a life event (such as having a new baby) or focus on the work at hand (finishing up that big report for work). As long as the stress does not harm the body and is temporary, it is not necessarily bad to experience. When it does become problematic, however, is when the stress is long term, ongoing, and results in negative physical and mental outcomes.

It is also important to note that stress is based on individual reactions to an event and that reactions may not be consistent between individuals. What develops as stress in one person will not emerge as stress in another.[2] As a result, stress is seen as transactional and lies in the encounter between the particular person and the particular event as people both influence and respond to their environment.[3]

Work-related stress is often experienced as a result of role conflict, role ambiguity, and role overload. In the case of nurturance suffering, each of these role issues is evident. Role conflict emerges because the distinction between teacher (only concerned with content) and counselor (concerned with emotional well-being with students) becomes blurred. While most teachers recognize that it is possible to take on both roles, there is still a limit to the capabilities in this area, which leads to role ambiguity; where does teaching content and students meet with addressing the emotional needs of students. Teachers realize that it is impossible to instruct content to a student who has emotional needs so great that he or she cannot concentrate. The home life and personal social lives of students do not stop at the classroom door. Role overload often occurs for teachers and manifests in nurturance suffering when the emotional needs of students are beyond the teacher's ability to assist.

Often with role conflict, it is difficult to identify the direct cause of stress as "individuals do not enact roles in isolation but in constellations, and strain is as likely to occur at the juncture of roles as within a role."[4] It is in this case that a teacher mixes roles. The professional training as a teacher will merge with societal expectations for women and men as well as with outside roles such as that of parent. It is not simply the role occupancy that creates the feeling of stress. Some teachers may teach for years and not experience or acknowledge nurturance suffering while others would target it as the primary cause of stress. It is the experiences and demands of the work and the role combined that establish the presence of stress. The variability will occur in how the individual perceives the role.[5]

This is also why it becomes difficult to compare the impact of nurturance suffering by gender simply based on the job definition as teacher. Many societal expectations by gender are also interwoven, yet not defined for that employment position. In some cases, it may be more difficult to identify nurturing suffering in men as although they may experience it, society does not allow them the flexibility to acknowledge it. The pressure to see nurturing as feminine coupled with the expectation that men should not display emotion creates a fragmented role conflict. For both genders, to admit stress is to admit failure.

Teaching requires "empathetic attention to the needs of others and the ability to provide emotional support to those in distress."[6] As it is typically women who are more likely to hold jobs characterized by stressful and nurturing conditions, they are often the ones most likely to bring the stress home and respond to family concerns with difficulty as they "already gave at the office."[7] It is women who are socialized to recognize the needs of others first in a nurturing manner. Regardless of the job position, women are expected to be supportive. Often it is this behavior that is linked to the role of mother, yet the act of being a mother is "rarely associated with psychological well-being and is often associated with psychological distress."[8] Women are socialized from birth to care for others and this contributes to the stress women experience. This greater range of caring exposes them to what Belle calls "vicarious stress."[9]

COPING

Knowing that teachers will experience this level of stress, why don't our teacher education programs, administration in-service training, and professional educators associations provide training for how to cope? Self-help techniques for dealing with stress became popular as early as the 1960s. Strategies such as exercise and relaxation techniques often were cited as simple ways to control stress. Now, it is time to bring these strategies out of the business world and high power careers such as medicine and law and into the classrooms so that teachers can benefit.

Before one can jump into a stress reduction program, however, one must first identify the causes of stress. It isn't always healthy to cope and sometimes the best solution is a career change. If the stress is ongoing, long term, and severe, perhaps there are greater factors at hand. Perhaps, this isn't the ideal career for the individual or perhaps it is the environment that is overwhelming and a change is in order. It is this level of stress that can quickly lead to burnout. If the stress is routine and short term (related to individual events or cases), coping may be the answer and that form of coping may include problem solving.

Typically, there are two types of coping mechanisms: those that focus on problem solving and those that focus on alleviating symptoms or manifestations of stress. Another coping style is appraisal based in which the individual redefines the problem. Appraisal coping may be beneficial when the problem cannot be problem solved; the individual truly wants to continue with the work and couples the appraisal with symptom relief.

For instance, in the case of nurturing suffering, the stress emerges as an agitation. It is a reaction triggered by the event of nurturing. Often, it is most likely a habit response to the stimulus of caring and while a reconditioning (appraisal approach) would be helpful, one does not want to turn off the response of caring altogether. The individual could redefine the issue by creating the understanding that although she wants to care for the student, she does not want the impact of that to extend outside of the school day. The individual remains nurturing, but creates a professional barrier or establishes a transition zone to keep the impact from going home with the grading at the end of the day. The individual could also redefine the stress from bad stress to good stress by recognizing that it is OK to care or worry and validating those feelings as being positive because they display a commitment to the students.

In addition, the individual can use exercise and mental imaging to relax at the end of the day before changing environments and arriving home. Problem solving may also be in order. The individual could ask the guidance teacher to take over or could help the student in taking steps to alleviate the core issue rather than just provide emotional support. Sometimes, it is the process of actually doing something to help, however small, that assists in alleviating the nurturance suffering.

The first step in alleviating your own school stress is to establish what is causing the stress. It may be advisable to keep a stress journal or diary. This will help identify several important pieces of information. In the stress journal, it is important to note stressful events and what occurred before the stressful reaction was recognized. Sometimes, it isn't until after the day has begun to close and we begin to relax that we recognize the tension we have held all day. Note the events of the day, what was occurring at the time of the feeling of stress and also the manifestation of the stress (was it physical such as a backache, psychological/emotional such as a crying jag or rage outburst, or was it social such as an avoidance of colleague gatherings). It is important to notice the patterns that occur because each of the three focus factors need to be considered and will need to be triaged using the three coping styles (problem solving, symptom relief, and appraisal).

After identifying the causes of stress, the emergence of stress, and the symptoms of stress, one can begin to apply the coping styles. This will be a trial and error time period. In addition, what may work one day, may not necessarily work the next.

Problem Solving

In order to problem solve, one must take a step back and objectively assess the situation. Consider if the stressful event is recurring and if it could be prevented in the future given changes in your behavior and responses to stimulus that cannot be controlled. For some people, this includes some very simple steps including problem-solving strategies.

For instance, a teacher is often overwhelmed on Fridays as the lesson plans are due to administration for untenured teachers on Friday. These lessons are always a problem for the teacher to generate and hand in. This teacher could use time management as a problem-solving strategy that would eliminate stress. Working a week ahead at all times would allow some flexibility in time and would prevent a feeling of stress when the plans are due. The weekend could be used to generate lessons that would be due the week after next. Because planning may shift due to snow days, field trips, or just a lesson that runs long, some quick adjustments might be needed, but the bulk of the work would be done. It seems a simple enough change to eliminate stress, but someone who is in the midst of stress might not see this as an easy change. Instead, this individual might blame an overintrusive administration or the tenure process. The individual might not think getting ahead is worth it because alterations may still be necessary.

Regardless of what the excuse making entails, problem solving requires one to let go of this and take an objective look to allow the individual to find a solution. Often taking a close look at one's own behavior and reactions is the most difficult step of the process. A close and trusted colleague who may help talk through the process could be beneficial in two ways. Not only can he help problem solve, but the colleague can also help with an emotional decompression of stress. Seeking support through a mentor can be very valuable and can provide the necessary information to process the stress event and begin to problem solve.

Symptom Relief

Often the situation cannot be resolved with problem solving and one must attempt to simply curtail the symptoms of stress that manifest. This is often the situation with nurturance suffering as teachers have very little power to effectively help a student with problems outside of the classroom. Symptoms could be physical, emotional, or social (see figure 2.1) and different strategies

Physical	Emotional	Social
Headache	Anger	Disconnect from
Twitching eyelid or other	Irritation	colleagues
facial muscle	Sadness/Crying	Avoidance of work events
Tense jaw	Moodiness	Withdraw from family
Ulcers	Depression	Lateness to work
Neck pain	Aggressive responses	Avoidance of work such
Back pain	Nightmares	as taking a sick day
Muscle aches	Anxiety	when not needed
Weakness	Feelings of panic	Avoidance while
Indigestion	Feelings of loss of control	at work—excessive
Nausea		e-mail checking,
Stomach pain		procrastination,
Digestion concerns/		nonparticipation in staff
diarrhea		meetings
Loss of appetite or		
overeating		
Insomnia		
Sweating		
Rapid breathing		

Behaviors:
Grinding teeth
Nervous tapping such as
foot or pen on table
Substance use such as
smoking or alcohol
Pacing
Change in food intake
Hair pulling or twirling
Cracking knuckles
Scowl on forehead or
pursed lips
Holding jaw tight
Nail biting
Chewing on lip

FIGURE 2.1
Common Reactions to Stress

may be used depending on the symptom and the individual's reaction to different strategies. Not every individual will react the same to stress stimuli and the response may differ day to day depending on the entire experience and not just the stress event.

Once triggers and stress responses are identified, one can target individual stress symptoms. The use of meditation, progressive muscle relaxation, and visualization can be very beneficial in alleviating stress. In extreme cases, a trip to the doctor for a checkup may also be in order to rule out larger health concerns or offer assistance in extreme issues such as in anxiety or depression. Some prefer the aid of a massage therapist or the use of exercise as a method for releasing or decompressing stress. Some people, for instance, walk to relieve stress. I often find that cleaning my house is stress relieving and provides a sense of reorder. Others prefer to talk with a peer group and release feelings of stress through dialogue. Another technique is creating zones in which the stress experienced at work can be left behind through the drive home or in errands such as stopping off at the grocery store. These are all healthy responses in order to alleviate stress.

Appraisal

Appraisal forces the individual to reexamine the stress event. In some instances, it simply requires a reframing of the understanding of the event in order to turn a negative into a positive. For those who suffer nurturance suffering, an appraisal understanding that the work is important and worthy may help alleviate the undue stress. Unfortunately, appraisal alone may have limited results as it does not alleviate the symptoms and offers little flexibility in solving the core issue. Another risk with using an appraisal strategy is that it may result in avoidance rather than true understanding.

Moos and Schaefer identify three types of appraisal for coping: logical analysis and mental preparation, cognitive redefinition, and cognitive avoidance or denial.[10] The focus of appraisal is to modify the meaning and comprehend the threat of any stress event.

Logical analysis and mental preparation requires the individual to break the stress event or problem into subcomponents that can make them more manageable. Rather than dealing with the overwhelming big picture, this step looks for all the elements that make up the larger event. It also requires the individual to draw on past successes in a self-coaching understanding and pairs this with mental imagining to prepare for what may come. For instance, let's return to our teacher who is overwhelmed with lesson planning once a week. Rather than focus on the large-scale stress (too much at once, accountability to an administrator that is resented for requiring the lessons in the first place, balancing unforeseen elements in the planning), the teacher could focus on just one piece at a time—perhaps beginning with the resentment of the administration. By resolving this and realizing that everyone who is nontenured is required to turn in plans and that the teacher is not a target by administration, the teacher can begin to focus on the true task at hand: time management. The teacher could also mentally prepare by taking time out of the quiet spaces that exist in the day to do some mental planning rather than to begin the draft in front of the computer with no preparation. The commute to work, the time in the shower, mowing the lawn, and other routine times are great spaces for mental imagery.

Cognitive redefinition recognizes that the situation cannot be resolved with problem solving and requires the individual to accept the reality of the stress event (either past or upcoming). The next step requires the individual to restructure the understanding of the problem into a more favorable understanding: a chance to be the optimist. This is also when the "well, it could be worse" point of view is valuable. The individual can focus on what good can come out of the situation. The teacher with a time crunch on lesson planning can see that he or she will benefit from the plans and that instruction has improved. He or she may also see that it has provided an opportunity to work on time management skills or even that next year will be better because one will be able to build on the work for this year. By doing this, the individual can adjust the perception to see the good and to see the comparison standard.

Cognitive avoidance or denial attempts to minimize the seriousness of a stress event. This provides no true coping as the problem will still exist once the diversion has reached a point where it no longer functions. Ignoring a problem will not make it go away and will in fact heighten the symptoms of stress. The teacher may be consistently late with lesson plans and then wonders why tenure was denied. Often blame is associated with this coping defense mechanism and the individual does not see how one's own culpability created or exacerbated the issue at hand.

Large-Scale Programs

I advocate the creation of larger scale programs for teachers to learn to cope with stress, particularly that of nurturance suffering. These programs can be integrated into teacher preparation programs, teacher in-service events such as superintendent days, professional development opportunities, and the structure of the faculty day.

The importance of the relationship between colleagues must be addressed within the field of education. Much like a family, colleagues who work closely together should capitalize on stress-reducing opportunities that could strengthen relationships and enhance the workplace. "Qualities such as open communication, empathy, emotional reassurance, support and sensitivity to each other's feelings characterize the therapeutic role."[11] This development should be fostered in teacher preparation capstone courses such as methods and student teaching seminar and can be continued right through one's years of teaching. Often schools create mentor programs for new teachers, which is an excellent first step, but these can be enhanced to create caring environments that are encouraged by administrators. This space could be much more effective if the teachers are trained in coping and listening strategies to better help each other.

Another avenue to take is stress inoculation programs initiated during the preservice years, which will provide future teachers a realistic understanding for what they may face in the field. Coupled with this realistic understanding, preservice teachers would receive direct instruction on recommendations for how to cope and problem solve for potential stress events such as would occur with nurturance suffering and the day-to-day business of teaching. The premise of stress inoculation is not a new idea and "the notion that people could be prepared for stress was very much in the air during World War II" through "battle inoculation."[12] This training included "films, pamphlets and illustrated lectures about the realities of combat dangers" and also included "gradual exposure to battle stimuli under reasonably safe conditions."[13] This sounds somewhat similar to student teaching programs, not that teaching is as intense as the battlefield of war, but teacher education programs often slowly introduce candidates to the field first through observation hours, then guided hours coupled with course work, and finally student teaching with a host teacher before gaining one's own classroom. The bulk of this time is spent on the logistics of teaching and not the emotions or resultant stress of teaching.

I have carried this theory into my own work with preservice methods and student teaching students. We discuss all of the elements of dealing with stress events starting with identifying the issue at hand and creating a plan for diffusing the stress. I also have set up online blogs for the students to keep in contact with each other while student teaching in order to foster a community of caring, which may not exist in their host public schools. In addition, I bring in a guest speaker who discusses stress and mental health with the students as we explore healthy ways to alleviate the stress encountered throughout the placements.

More specific plans can also be used. There are a number of texts available that promote ways in which an individual can alleviate stress. Carrington (1984), for instance, has created a "releasing" method in which individuals can target stress the moment it is experienced.[14] The act of releasing teaches the stressed individual to let go of emotional strain by monitoring stressful situations, considering the possibilities, and actively choosing another emotional response other than stress. A key element of this technique is recognizing when one has control in order to act and when one does not have control of the situation. This method combines many of the strategies of problem solving, symptom relief, and appraisal in one quick assessment.

NOTES

1. Carry L. Cooper and Philip Dewe, *Stress: A Brief History* (Malden, Mass.: Blackwell Publishing, 2004), 11.

2. Ibid., 68.

3. Donald Miechenbaum and Matt E. Jaremko, eds., *Stress Reduction and Prevention* (New York: Plenum Press, 1983), 101.

4. Carol S. Aneshensel and Leonard I. Pearlin, "Structural Contexts of Sex Differences in Stress," in *Gender and Stress*, eds. Rosalind Barnett, Lois Biener, and Grace K. Baruch (New York: Free Press, 1987), 57.

5. Ibid., 83.

6. Deborah Belle, "Gender Differences in the Social Moderators of Stress," in *Gender and Stress*, eds. Rosalind Barnett, Lois Biener, and Grace K. Baruch (New York: Free Press, 1987), 265.

7. Ibid.

44

CHAPTER 2

8. Rosalind Barnett and Grace K. Baruch, "Social Roles, Gender, and Psychological Distress," in *Gender and Stress*, eds. Rosalind Barnett, Lois Biener, and Grace K. Baruch (New York: Free Press, 1987), 132.

9. Belle, "Gender Differences in the Social Moderators of Stress," 268.

10. Rudolf H. Moos and Jeanne A. Schaefer, "Life Transitions and Crisis: A Conceptual Overview," in *Coping with Life Crisis: An Integrated Approach*, ed. Rudolf H. Moos (New York: Plenum Press 1986), 14–16.

11. Denise A. Skinner, "Dual-Career Family Stress and Coping," in *Coping with Life Crisis: An Integrated Approach*, ed. Rudolf H. Moos (New York: Plenum Press 1986), 110.

12. Irving L. Janis, "Stress Inoculation in Health Care: Theory and Research," in *Stress Reduction and Prevention*, eds. Donald Miechenbaum and Matt E. Jaremko (New York: Plenum Press, 1983), 68.

13. Ibid.

14. Patricia Carrington, *Releasing: The New Behavioral Science Method for Dealing with Pressure Situations* (New York: William Morrow and Company, Inc., 1984).

3

Case Studies

What follow are a short series of case studies. Each case study is focused on a particular teacher population and/or reaction for handling job-related stress. Keep in mind that these are composites of several teachers in each case study and that you may find elements of your own experiences in several of the studies although you may not fit the overall identifier of the case study main character.

ANA—THE ESTABLISHED TEACHER

Ana, an experienced teacher, still experiences stress. In many of the examples, this stress is related to nurturance suffering, but she also is subject to the many job-related stresses that plague teachers on a daily basis. Ana, unlike many teachers, has had some training in how to cope with stress as she has a background in guidance counseling.

School days are often routine and Ana is prepared to handle routine. She knows that throughout her day there will be minor stressful events, which she has developed coping mechanisms for in order to alleviate stress during the day rather than to allow it to build up and go home with her. For instance, she knows that she needs to take at least a half an hour at the end of the school day to organize for the next day and shuffle through paperwork. If she doesn't, this leaves an even bigger pile the next day and she will begin her day in a foul mood.

She also knows that during the day she will sometimes become agitated due to a class or student concern and she can help alleviate that during the day by walking and doing errands in the building during her planning period. Not every day is so easily managed however and in the case study below, Ana experiences a stressful event that she does not have a ready solution for.

Case Study Vignette

Ana often sat with a few other teachers for lunch. They met in Ana's classroom, which was closest to the lunch room, and today like many other days, the teachers began by talking about their mornings. They often had complaints, but also other news such as plans for the upcoming vacation. Ana joined the group and placed her tray of baked ziti in front of her. Wishing momentarily that she had bought a salad instead, Ana sighed and picked up her fork. Gwen, the biology teacher, sat to her left and was talking about a tenth grade student, Katie.

As Ana listened to the conversation, she began to make connections in the stories that the teachers were sharing about Katie. The teachers often talked about students as a way of comparing stories and trying to find a way to best help students, but in this case, they needed more help than they could provide in their classrooms. Katie was an average student with a warm smile. She was friendly with the teachers and most other students. Ana had Katie in her homeroom the year before and she still came to say good morning every day. Now Ana had her in the third period career preparation course that Ana taught. Everyone had started noticing changes in Katie's behavior, and another student, Nicky, who was in Katie's class, had gone to a teacher with concerns that morning.

"Apparently, this boy comes here during lunch," Gwen was saying to the table. "I tried talking to her yesterday and she just kept saying everything was fine. That she was tired and hadn't been sleeping."

"When did all this happen anyway?" asked the guidance counselor. "I thought she was dating Josh."

"She was, but then they split up and she started dating this Show kid." No one actually knew the boy's name, not even Nicky and he was Katie's closest friend at school. They all just referred to him by the nickname that Katie used, Show. That morning, Nicky had gone to Gwen in order to ask for help on behalf of Katie. He waited until the room was empty and told Gwen everything he knew: that Show had hurt Katie, grabbed her arm in school one day, shoved her down a set of bleachers last week, and bought her alcohol on a regular basis.

"Well, if he is coming here at lunch, can't they just not let him in the building? We have a sign in and that is the only door you can come through." Ana was starting to get angry with the frustration and futility of the situation.

"One would think . . . but then again, it happens all the time. People just walk in and aren't questioned. Sometimes security isn't even there." Gwen lifted a forkful of the ziti.

"That needs to be taken up with admin then. That's unacceptable." Ana leaned forward on the table and gestured with her soda bottle. Her face was starting to turn red and blotchy as she thought of the whole situation. Knowing that they had a staff meeting that afternoon, Ana was already planning her selection of words. Students started coming into the room and the teachers quickly changed the topic of conversation.

Later at the staff meeting, Ana brought up the situation with Katie and received a noncommittal response from the principal. A simple "We will look into it" was all he would say. He did promise to remind the front desk security to have people sign in and to not leave the desk unattended. Knowing that the teachers are mandated reporters, he said he would take it up with guidance, but when pressed would not say more. He argued that the teachers had not seen anything happen and were only going on the reports of another student.

As Ana had stayed late to clean off her desk, she was still in the building when Celeste, the guidance counselor, came by Ana's room. She had left the staff meeting early to call Katie's mother and wanted to give an update to Ana.

"Don't you ever go home?" Celeste laughed as she opened the door.

"Some days, it doesn't seem like it. Did you talk to Katie's mother?" Ana set down the pile of papers she had in her hand.

"Yes, and Katie denied everything. She said she made it up to get attention."

"She told her mother that?" Ana shouldn't have been surprised but couldn't help it. She had hoped that Katie would have more support at home. "And her mother believed it?"

"Yup, total buy in. Told us not to worry and that she would keep an eye on her just in case." Celeste's voice dripped with sarcasm. It was obvious from her tone that she thought if Katie's mom had kept an eye on her in the first place this wouldn't be an issue now.

Ana wrapped up the conversation and then picked up a book in distraction. Seconds later, she set it down a little harder than anticipated and the heavy *thunk* on her desk shifted loose papers drifting to the floor in a manner so peaceful that it further irritated Ana. Falling papers should match the mood. Ana assumed that Katie wouldn't be alright. She was looking for help; otherwise, she wouldn't have told Nicky. Katie had managed to put on a false impression of strength, but she was frayed at the edges and her voice showed it. Another day gone and another frustration to add to the collection. Ana couldn't help thinking about Katie the whole drive home and every scenario that Ana played in her mind still ended with Katie in trouble.

Review

Ana attempts to use the problem-solving technique throughout her narrative. She uses the resources of the principal and of Celeste (the guidance counselor) to help her assess the precipitating stress event more clearly and to seek a resolution. In this situation, Ana is able to maintain a balance with smaller and routine stress events. She uses positive coping techniques such as walking and talking with peers in order to alleviate stress. She also plans ahead to manage potential stress and forces herself to stay a bit later in the day to organize for the next day and prevent a bad morning.

In the case of Katie, there is little she can do. This is a case of nurturance suffering and her stressful reaction is worsened with what appears to be an unsupportive administration and her own lack of control over the situation. The principal's reaction only makes Ana more frustrated because of the lack of support and she takes the problem home with her. Usually, Ana likes to try to box off her home stress and school stress and leave one behind as she enters a new environment. In this case, she was unable to do that and one will undoubtedly affect the other. Ana also feels powerless in her position and feels as if she can't effectively help a student in need.

Consider This

Ana uses the lunch period to decompress her stress load by talking with peers. Most days this is beneficial and she can lessen the stress that has built up over the course of the morning. Other teachers who join the conversation also share their concerns, so there is reciprocal care in support of one another.

Do you have a support network that you can share with? Ideally, this network would be others who are familiar with the setting, but it can also be individuals apart from the school environment who can listen to your thoughts without preconceived notions about the individuals you would know in common. If you don't have a network, how can you begin one? If you do have a network, consider if this network is really supportive or just appears that way. Consider the teacher's lounge for instance—this is not always the most positive environment of the school and may heighten the stress rather than alleviate it.

Ana finds an unsupportive administration in her principal. Sometimes, it is helpful to examine the situation from the opposite point of view. Perhaps he is supportive but unable to voice any judgments as he too is limited in what actions he can take. We cannot control the level of support we receive from administration, and sometimes it is helpful to examine why a particular level has been offered rather than become angry and assume that the reaction is just from a lack of concern. Ana does not consider these other mitigating factors and focuses only on her limited power in the situation.

Can you think of a time when you wanted to help a student but were limited by outside forces? Did this cause you emotional stress and emerge as nurturance suffering? Rethink that situation now that time has passed; were there perhaps other factors in play at the time? Consider elements such as role conflict. Perhaps this is the true cause of the dramatic reaction to the stressful event. When we expect people to react out of role or we ourselves react out of role, stress can emerge or be exacerbated. Ana expects the principal to immediately react, but as a principal, he must collect all the data he can before jumping to a reaction. He also knows that the reports are secondhand and not directly from Katie and were not observed by the teachers. He is limited in his ability to respond; yet Ana expects immediate action.

Usually, Ana can separate work from home. It is often difficult for people to do this. Ana does this by providing transition spaces such as the quiet time in her classroom after the day is over and during her long drive home. These transition spaces allow Ana to decompress the stress that has built up over the day. What transition spaces do you use to help you move from one environment to another and how do you use this time to help alleviate stress? If you do not already do this, where might opportunities to create transition spaces occur? Consider running errands after school, getting a cup of coffee, or as Nathan from the third case study does, playing a game of basketball with friends. Keep in mind that you want to create a positive transition space—one that is healthy. Some transition spaces may be harmful.

GABRIELLE—AN EARLY CAREER TEACHER

Gabrielle is an English teacher in her third year of teaching. She teaches eleventh and twelfth grade at an alternative high school in a small urban setting. Gabrielle often experiences stress as a result of her teaching and interactions with students. She worries about her teaching and strives to be someone that students can connect with. She also places great value on how students react to her and wants students to value her. Gabrielle is a social person and often chats with other teachers throughout the school day. She does not like that her classroom prevents her from easily talking with other adults.

Case Study Vignette

Gabrielle dressed comfortably and her dress reflects her personality and her teacher style. Fashion appeared to be important to her and she often spoke to the students about current trends. Today, she wore a black sheath dress that ended at her knees and she paired it with matching black heeled sandals and dark rimmed glasses. Her short blond hair framed her face and her highlights accented her light tan. Gabrielle appears healthy and she is high energy. She is in good spirits today and jokes easily with her students as they enter her English class.

One of the first students through the door begins to immediately complain about the reading he had for homework and Gabrielle, determined not to let him bother her, shakes her head with a smile. Her silver drop earrings dangle and sway with the movement, catching the florescent lighting from above.

"Well, you still have to get it done. The next six weeks are really important." The school year is beginning to wind down and the pressure of year-end exams weighs on both the students and the teachers.

Another student, Dion, chimes in with her interpretation of the correct way to complete the homework. She says that all she did was read the last chapter. After all, she says, all the important stuff happens in the last chapter.

Gabrielle is obviously not impressed with this response and draws an imaginary circle around her thin face with an acrylic French manicured nail. "See this face," she says. "This is me not smiling. I am not amused."

Gabrielle continues the class and the block schedule period moves on with little hassle. The students complete their reading and at the close of the period Gabrielle reminds them of the next assignments. Later, she leaves for her quick lunch break and a fellow English teacher accompanies her on a short drive down the hill and around the block. There is just enough time to smoke a cigarette down the hill and another on the way back. The tan leather seats of her Jeep are hot from the sun beaming down through the front windshield and the leather smells warm; the neatness of the vehicle would not suggest one who smokes. It does not smell of cigarette smoke and her ashtray is unused. Along the way, Gabrielle discusses the morning's events and flicks her ash out the window.

"You know, when I was a kid, I never would have dared say that to a teacher. I would have been too afraid to disappoint them." Gabrielle continues to reflect on the tale of Dion and her last chapter theory of reading homework. The light turns red at the end of the hill and the Jeep idles while the two teachers compare notes on annoying things high school students say.

The two teachers then begin to discuss the novels they are teaching and Gabrielle comments that she wished she had started teaching this one earlier. The novel includes some sexually graphic scenes and uses some harsh language. Although she has taught the novel in the past, she comments that she is concerned with the reactions of one student and the reactions his family may have. She discusses ideas on how to approach the topic with her colleague, and as they share ideas, Gabrielle often nods or chimes in with comments such as "I'll try that" and "maybe that will work."

It appears that the two teachers share the burden of daily stress and they compare short stories of the day's events and worries for the remainder of the day. When they return to school and use Gabrielle's ID badge to enter the building, both appear refreshed and ready to take on their afternoon classes.

Review

Gabrielle does attempt to find spaces within the day to decompress her stress load. She also has a small network to commiserate and problem solve with. Unfortunately, Gabrielle often resorted to unhealthy responses. Avoidance through smoking may provide temporary relief, but once the distracter has been removed, the stress will return, often in the quiet hours before sleep thus causing insomnia. Gabrielle would have benefited much more from a healthy technique that would have a lasting impact. In addition, the technique she chose could not be brought into the workplace. A technique such as cleansing breaths would have been more fitting.

She also anticipates stress, which has both benefits and drawbacks. In anticipating a conflict over the content of a novel, she is able to prepare a response or attempt to find a way to eliminate it as a problem before it can emerge. As a drawback, she is allowing herself to become concerned when there may not ever be a problem. It is a good idea to anticipate problems as long as one is able to problem solve and let a concern drop to the side until it does manifest as a problem. Some people are not able to do this and will fixate on a problem before it even emerges and create stress that is nonexistent.

Due to Gabrielle's social nature, she benefits most from decompressing stress by chatting with others. The "motel-like configuration" described by DeMarrais and LeCompte (1999) is modeled in Gabrielle's school. There are four main wings to the building and construction will soon begin on an addition to the school. Classrooms follow a traditional style in that each teacher has a classroom with an entrance to a common hallway. Looking down the hall, one gets the image of a motel with a series of doors leading to environments in which there is typically one teacher. This does not allow for much interaction with peers throughout the school day. This leads to a sense of disconnectedness and isolation for Gabrielle and impacts her stress levels. Luckily, Gabrielle has managed to avoid a pitfall of many teachers in this situation in that she chats with a peer at lunch about the work. Often, teachers participate in a pioneer ethic in which they feel as if they must do their work alone. This pioneer ethic encourages teachers to work individually and to not complain as a complaint may be viewed as a weakness.

Consider This

Many people respond to stress with unhealthy ways of coping. Smoking and avoidance techniques like television watching are not healthy. Another common unhealthy coping skill is holding the transition time between school and work in an environment that is not beneficial. Individuals for instance who go to a bar after work multiple times a week could better make use of this transition time, which is currently nonproductive and avoidance behavior.

Other unhealthy responses can include overeating or withdrawing from others. Some people also withdraw from the work both emotionally and physically when faced with stress. All of these reactions to stress build on an avoidance tactic. Think of your own responses to stress. Are they positive coping strategies that help you to continue to work in a healthy manner or are they negative strategies that hinder your ability to handle stress? Often, we fail to see our own reactions to stress as negative or in some cases fail to see the connection as a reaction at all. Television watching for instance can be a healthy way (when in moderation) to relax and participate in a form of entertainment. If, however, one watches television to avoid facing problems that will still be present after the screen goes dark, the activity is not healthy.

The additional problem for Gabrielle is her dislike of the isolation created by the configuration of the classrooms. Knowing that the configuration cannot be changed, what can a teacher do to heighten the connection to colleagues? One solution is collaborative team teaching. Gabrielle built into her lesson plans opportunities to team teach interdisciplinary lessons with several of the other teachers in the building. Not only did this benefit students, but she was able to benefit by strengthening a sense of community in her building and connecting more to her peer teachers. Another way to avoid the sense of isolation is by standing in the hall door during the time between classes. This not only benefits students as you greet them entering the room, but also helps manage discipline in the hall and provides an opportunity to see and greet other teachers. Eating lunch with peer teachers and organizing other group activities such as a holiday lunch for teachers or a basketball group also helps develop that sense of connection to peer teachers. Consider opportunities to team teach a lesson or unit and try to team with colleagues in other nonprofessional-related activities such as starting a book club that could meet after school in a local coffee shop. The change in environment may help you better connect with your colleagues and create a community and supportive environment at work.

NATHAN—MIDDLE SCHOOL TEACHER WITH TENURE

Nathan, like the first case study, Ana, identifies as a nurturing teacher. He connects with and cares for his middle school students beyond just the class period of instruction. He is also involved with community-related projects that he connects to his classroom work. Nathan is successful in his classroom but is often frustrated by other forces such as budgets that limit his ability to purchase materials for his art classroom. He is also frustrated by his administration and the quick turnover in leadership. The school has had four principals in six years. He also has differences in educational philosophy in comparison with the current principal and does not agree with some of the policies in place. When faced with this stress, Nathan often reacts with anger and feelings of irritation.

Case Study Vignette

The school day has closed and Nathan steps out of his classroom and walks over to the current gym classroom. Inside are ping pong tables for the current unit and Nathan picks up a paddle.

"No way are you going to beat me today." Marc, the PE teacher, steps out of his office laughing and walks up to the table.

"Really?" Nathan spins his paddle. "Not like how I schooled you in basketball yesterday?" After the school day, Nathan, Marc, and another male teacher often find time to hang out. Sometimes it is a quick game of ping pong before the staff meeting, but typically it is a longer game of basketball after the other teachers have gone home for the day.

The two men begin to play and Nathan plays with vigor. They laugh and tease each other throughout the game. After only moments of play, two other teachers join to watch and one challenges the soon-to-be winner. As is custom, the group of teachers begin to talk about their day and one complains about a new policy that the administration has put in place.

"I know it." Nathan turns to the conversation. "Seriously, they need to limit the crap these kids take in every day and they would behave better. Soda machines should not be in the building—it doesn't matter if you say they just can't have it until after noon."

"Doesn't matter," Marc who also teaches health chimes in. "When they aren't drinking soda, they have their pockets stuffed with junk food that they get from the vending machine or whatever candy bar or lollipop sale is going on."

"No, what doesn't matter is that in ten minutes when we go to the staff meeting to complain about the memo that came out without ever talking to the teachers, we will get the same response we always get . . . 'it is in the best interests of the students, blah, blah, we will evaluate it after it has been in place.' And then in two months, they will hope we have all forgotten about it and in the meantime three new things to be concerned with will pop up." Nathan, having lost the match, gives up his paddle to the next teacher in line.

At that point, the announcement came on requesting teachers to move to the cafeteria for the staff meeting. A collective groan went up among the teachers. Staff meetings rarely seemed beneficial and they were always the same format. The administration went through their list of announcements and then left only a few minutes for the teachers to voice concerns. Then, these concerns were quickly forgotten by the administration as soon as the meeting broke up.

As the teachers headed to the meeting, they continued to chat about the day and Nathan shared a concern he had about a student. The student had continued to withdraw from the other students and now was no longer turning in class assignments. Nathan had a good rapport with the student and knew that something was wrong, but was unable to find out what. Worried about the student and unhappy with recent budget constraints, Nathan was glad for the small ping pong break the teachers had managed to work into the end of the day. Sadly, with the upcoming meeting any stress relief he had experienced during the game was about to evaporate.

Review

Nathan does a great job of creating transition spaces to prevent bringing stress home. The transition space of playing basketball with some of the other teachers after teaching helps him alleviate stress and separate the school day from home. This healthy transition allows him to return home refreshed and ready to continue his work. He can't play basketball every day though and needs to develop more transitions on the other three days a week. The ping pong games are a great start for this, but they are squeezed in between the end of class and the start of the staff meeting. Any benefit is quickly erased as Nathan dreads going to meetings and his mind-set is that the meetings are not positive.

By doing an appraisal and perspective change, Nathan may begin to view staff meetings as more positive. An appraisal allows Nathan to redefine the stress triggers. Rather than placing blame on the administration in that "they don't take teachers' views into consideration," he can redefine the problem as, "I need to voice my concerns in a less attacking manner that may put off administration." If that doesn't work, he can continue to redefine the problem and problem solve until the situation is resolved or he must admit that this is an irresolvable problem. When faced with irresolvable stress, he has several

options, many of which may not be ones he is willing to accept as they would
impact his classroom teaching, which is successful. Leaving the position or
beginning to shut down from participation outside his own classroom would
help manage his stress, but they may not be beneficial choices as both options
would impact his career and may also be viewed as defeatist.

Consider This

The mind-set that one brings to an event will alter the response one has to
the event. If you dread staff meetings then chances are that you will not find
them beneficial and a positive experience. Changing the mind-set may be a
first step in alleviating stress. One part of Nathan's dread probably comes
from the quick turnover the school has had in principals. This does not allow
for any real working relationship to develop between the staff and the teachers. The teachers in turn begin to see the administration as unsupportive and
in Nathan's case giving top-down directives without teacher input.

In some cases, the problem is more severe and can't be resolved with a
change in perspective. In this case, problem solving may help provide solutions to create a better work environment. When the situation is so hostile
however that the work environment becomes toxic and the individual experiences severe mental and physical stress, manifestations that may lead to
burnout, one should consider a change in environment.

DEVONTE—FIRST YEAR TEACHER AT A MAGNET SCHOOL

Devonte often feels as if his peers view him as a kid because he is younger. He
often feels as if he can't contribute to staff meetings and other professional
situations as the response he hears is, "We tried that two years ago and it
didn't work." As a result, Devonte began to shut down at meetings and began
to believe that his teaching methods and ideas were best kept to himself. His
mentor, assigned by the school as part of a new initiative to help new teachers
adjust, notices the change. In addition, like many new teachers, Devonte worries about continuing his education and beginning a master's degree.

Case Study Vignette

Devonte sat at his desk watching the clock tick and counted the moments
until 3:15 when he could leave—released from another day at work. He felt
like a student sometimes in this way, as if school was something he was forced

to do and not something he loved. He was exhausted both mentally and physically from the work and at times wondered if it was worth it. He enjoyed the students and his classes but was unable to connect to the other teachers.

Sighing and packing his bag with his grading that needed to be done and the materials he needed to plan for the next day, Devonte wondered how he would ever get past the paper load. It seemed as if every night he had work to do. Just as he was about to add in the textbook, Ben, his assigned mentor, entered the room. Devonte glanced at the clock again, 3:07—hopefully, this wouldn't take long.

"How's it going?" Ben asked, settling himself uncomfortably into one of the small desks for the students. "Noticed you didn't sign up to lead a table for curriculum night." Curriculum night was a contract requirement and amounted to an open house for parents except with the addition of fair tables that the teachers ran to talk about things like the school dress code policy and school philosophy.

"I figured it would be best if I didn't. It's not like I know all the policies anyway." Devonte crossed an arm over his chest and began to rub his shoulder. He had a permanent knot that he could not work out and it became irritated just about every day.

"No one expects you to recite the school mission statement verbatim. It would be good to get more involved with the other teachers." Ben paused, "How's that success file going?" Noticing that Devonte was starting to drag midyear, Ben had suggested that Devonte begin to keep a file to record his successes.

"Good. I added a photo yesterday of our class projects." Devonte had not done this, but it sounded like a good answer. How was he going to find time to organize that when he was struggling just to put together a lesson plan for the next day?

Review

Devonte struggles with the most common stressors for new teachers. Trying to fit in with colleagues and keep up with the paper load were constant pressures. His reactions to this stress emerge in two ways. First, he wants to escape the environment and looks forward to the end of the day as a means of bringing relief. This is a social reaction that prevents him from becoming more a part of the professional community of teachers.

His second reaction is a physical reaction to the stress in that he develops a pain in his shoulder. This may be in part due to how he holds his body posture when stressed. He may lift his shoulders toward his ears in a defensive and tense posture. This localized tension may also be exacerbated with improper body posture at the computer or at his desk when correcting papers and writing lesson plans. If this is not addressed, it may result in chronic back pain. This type of physical pain can further disrupt his ability to deal with stress and may lead to feeling a loss of control. Chronic pain of this sort is typically the result of repetitive stress reaction body positioning and he must be willing to identify the cause rather than just treat the symptoms. While a visit to a massage therapist will provide relief, it will only be temporary if Devonte continues the same path of stress and body posture response. Other types of stress reactions that may result in physical pain and discomfort can include holding the jaw tense, chewing on the lip, grinding the teeth, scowling, and stomach discomfort due to stressful eating habits.

Devonte also continues to enhance his stress levels due to a lack of risk taking. By being shut down at early meetings when voicing opinions, he has resorted to keeping silent and withdrawn from participation. This social avoidance while at work will only make his stress levels worse as he begins to feel isolated from his peers and more disconnected. Devonte should take his mentor's advice and participate more in the curriculum night by hosting a table. Perhaps, there is a position he would be more comfortable with such as running the front table where parents are greeted as they enter. By doing this, he will be able to connect with the other teachers in a more social way and he will be able to feel as if he is contributing to the school. He will also begin to feel as if he is gaining more control over his environment.

Consider This

Learning from his mentor, Devonte eventually began to keep a file folder of notes, cards, and other artifacts that reminded him why he went into teaching. He included a holiday card from a student, a thank you e-mail from a parent, and even photographs of him working with students on successful projects. Other items could include positive evaluations from his principal, a copy of the script from the school play that he helped sell tickets for, and a note to himself about what went well that year. A success file reminds us why we stay in teaching and reminds us that we are appreciated and what we do matters.

If you have already started a success file—that's great. What else can you add to it? If you haven't, you may want to consider starting a simple file folder. Mine got too large for a file folder and I moved it all to a decorative memory box I picked up at an inexpensive craft store. Over the years, I have saved a lot of random items from students and coworkers that remind me that the work I do is valued.

Because of Devonte's physical reaction to stress, he may also want to consider visiting a massage therapist and using progressive muscle relaxation. Evaluate your body positioning and bring awareness to your posture when you experience stress. Feel for where you carry tension and focus on relaxing this muscle or muscle group. It may be helpful to create a saying to recite when you are stressed once you identify where you carry tension. For instance, Devonte upon initially beginning to feel stressed can force himself to drop his arms to his sides and can ask himself to relax his shoulders. Coupled with a cleansing breath, Devonte can recenter himself. As this can be a silent message voiced inside his head, Devonte can use this method when in direct contact with the stressful situation.

Think of a cue that you can use to let go of a situation and release stress before you tense up. Devonte, when beginning to tense his upper back and jaw as a result of stress, could drop his hands to his lap and focus on trying to relax his shoulders. Usually, one should only have to do this for a moment to recenter. Often one may find that as soon as he or she refocuses on the task at hand he or she will begin to tense up again. It is important to build this relaxation into the body posture routine in order to break this cycle.

Devonte benefits from a mentor who is assigned by the school to assist Devonte in his transition to the new school and his position as a new teacher. While many schools do this, some do not, and it may be advantageous for you to select your own mentor. In the event that your school has assigned you one, you may still want to seek out another that may benefit you. Select an individual that you can trust and speak easily with. Keep in mind that although it may be helpful if this mentor is in your content area, it is not a requirement to finding a great mentor. A great mentor can guide you in the school policies and paperwork, help you develop your teaching rapport with other staff, and help you problem solve. It is a great mentor who can help you talk through a situation to find answers rather than immediately suggesting quick fixes. The goal is to find someone who can help you talk through a problem in order to discover a solution or a series of potential solutions. Mentors are also available for witnessing your successes as well and to help you celebrate milestones you make in your early years of teaching.

JENNIFER—STUDENT TEACHER

As required by her college, Jennifer needed to complete two student teaching placements to graduate. One was in a middle school setting and the second was with a high school class. As a result, she had three people she had to work with: her seminar teacher, her supervising teacher from the college that came to observe her, and her cooperating teacher of the placement. And as luck would have it, each person had a different set of requirements and expectations, including teaching methods and lesson plan format. She felt as if she were torn in different directions trying to make everyone happy. In addition, Jennifer feels as if the students do not look at her as the "real teacher" and she feels that this leads to classroom management problems. She feels undermined by her cooperating teacher during the school day in that students when told no by Jennifer will turn to the cooperating teacher to get a different answer.

Case Study Vignette

Already running behind in the lesson for the day, Jennifer silently screams inside her head. She can see her cooperating teacher in the back of the room shaking her head as if in dismay that Jennifer is once again blowing a lesson plan. Of course, it didn't help that Jennifer had to write three versions to make everyone happy.

"Miss Kleer?" Jennifer looks up to see a student in the back of the room wildly waving his hand in the air.

"Yes, Jacob?" Jennifer hesitantly asks as she turns to hand out papers to the front row of students. Jacob has had a history of trying to get class off topic and often asks ridiculous questions. Jennifer worries that he is doing it just to torment her and embarrass her hoping she won't have an answer. What she doesn't know is that he does this with all his teachers, including her cooperating teacher.

"Can I use the computer for this essay?" A simple enough question for a change and Jennifer answers no, that everyone should do the essay at their desk as it is only a page and due by the end of the class period. Jacob frowns and turns behind him to the cooperating teacher. Repeating his question,

Jacob is pleased that the second answer is a yes, and he picks up his materials to move to the back of the room. Inwardly, Jennifer groans. Once again, her response is thwarted by the cooperating teacher. Of course, in reaction to Jacob using the computer, three other students want to move as well.

Jennifer somehow manages to make it through the rest of the class and collects the papers as students head on to third period. Glad she doesn't teach third period, she moves to her small table in the back corner with the essays.

"Jennifer, a moment." The cooperating teacher calls Jennifer over with a wave of her hand. "Let's examine that lesson before you begin grading." As the teacher talks, Jennifer begins to fade out and listen to the inner dialogue she has running in her head. She nods at all the right pauses in the critique of her lesson, but what Jennifer is really thinking about is how much she feels out of control. She is reminded every day that she isn't the real teacher, that this isn't her classroom, and that she doesn't know what she is doing. No one tells her these things, but with such harsh criticism from her cooperating teacher, she can't help but feel this way.

It doesn't help that she isn't sleeping at night. She lies awake staring at the ceiling after a long night of preparation for the next day and worries that her lesson won't go well, that there will be classroom management problems, and that she won't have enough cash in her wallet to last the week and pay for gas.

Review

Jennifer knew going into her student teaching experience that it would be difficult and a change from just attending classes. However, she was not prepared for the difficulties that would arise during the experience. Her own feelings of inadequacy have left her self-esteem low and she is frustrated by the limited control she has over the class and the lessons. Another difficulty Jennifer has is that she does not communicate her concerns with her cooperating teacher and supervising teacher. Rather than voice her concerns when the cooperating teacher talks with her about the lesson, Jennifer fades out and begins to have a side conversation inside her head rather than focus on the commentary and participate in the dialogue. She could also have spoken to the three instructors she works with: her cooperating teacher, supervision teacher, and seminar teacher in order to resolve the concern she has with lesson planning and format. It is doubtful that all three teachers would be inflexible on the format and Jennifer should be able to find common ground so that she need not write three plans every time.

Jennifer also needs to take a close look at her time management and sleeping schedule. Late nights working and worrying are detrimental to her ability to cope with the following day. A muscle relaxation activity prior to bed may be beneficial for Jennifer. She should also try to keep a set schedule for sleeping rather than vary her routine. During the student teaching phase of their schooling preservice teachers are often comfortable with late nights, but not as comfortable with early mornings. Trying to find balance and alter one's sleeping pattern from a full-time college student to a working professional may be a challenge. She also needs to find a way of releasing her fears for the next day and the future in order to sleep. There are many tips she could try, including meditation, a limit on caffeine in the evening, sticking to a routine (even on the weekend), and prioritizing tasks.

Other factors such as television watching prior to bed and working in bed can harm one's sleep schedule. The bedroom should not be a place for grading and other paperwork. It can be an attractive idea to lie in bed and grade papers in a comfortable position, but then the mind begins to consider this a work environment and not a relaxing environment. Jennifer wants to avoid thinking of work before sleep in order to get back to a more appropriate sleep schedule and needs to begin to make changes in order to achieve this goal.

Consider This

Examine the level of control you have over your own environment. Consider the classroom, the school as a whole, any committees you are on, and your home life. In each instance, rate how in control you feel from a 1 (not in control) to a 5 (most in control). Then consider the individual situations. In some cases, not being in control isn't necessarily a bad thing. For instance, in joining a new committee with a task you are unfamiliar with, it may be best not to be in control. This is difficult for some people as they do not want to relinquish control over situations. In other cases, it is extremely important to have a balance of power and control over the environment such as in the home and within your own classroom. For Jennifer, it would inappropriate for her to have complete control over the classroom as she is a student teacher; however, there should be some balance in order for her to have effective classroom management.

Look back on your list of environments and how in control you feel. Where are you comfortable giving up control and where on your list are environments in which you need to gain more control? Consider ways in which you can become more in control over the environment: speaking to those with whom you need to share control may be a first step, but the ability to be more assertive may also be called for in the environment in order to make a change.

Also, step back and take a look at your sleeping habits. Do you keep a consistent schedule? Are you working from your bed? Are you participating in other activities, such as having caffeine after 7 pm, that may impact your ability to sleep? If you are keeping a stress diary as advised earlier, you should also begin to pay particular attention to the hours before attempting to sleep to track any poor habits you may have that will impact your ability to fall asleep and stay asleep. I would not advise the use of medication unless the problem is persistent and you have tried alternatives such as meditation first. Only under the direction of a doctor should one consider the use of sleeping medication for severe insomnia.

If you are considerate of the poor habits that may impact your sleep and you have tried meditation and muscle relaxation but find that you are still unable to fall asleep at a beneficial time at night, take a look at your past sleep schedule. As a full-time college student, did you plan to sleep at midnight each night and now you are trying to fall asleep at ten? In this case you have established a sleep schedule that is no longer beneficial to your need to be up at 6 am to teach for the day. Perhaps an herbal supplement of melatonin for a short time coupled with a set bedtime and a commitment to follow other helpful bedtime routines can get you back on track and reset your body clock. This is not a permanent solution however, and although an herbal supplement is available at many stores, the use of this remedy should still be discussed with a physician.

MARTHA BETH—SIX-YEAR TEACHER

Martha Beth loves teaching her high school students. She especially loves when the work she does is validated by students who reciprocate in caring. Martha Beth often runs out of time in the day to do everything on her lists. She is often stressed and exhibits stress-related symptoms such as a feeling of anxiety and nervousness, but she isn't sure why as she is happy in her career as a teacher.

Case Study Vignette

Martha Beth, after dropping off her bag and coat, headed to the main office to clean out her mailbox. Every morning she has the same routine and has used this routine for the past several years. A trip to the office to get her mail and chat a bit, a stop by the teacher's lounge for a cup of coffee, and back to her room to check her e-mail until homeroom begins. Then, during homeroom, she puts up the agenda for the day's classes.

Martha Beth set down her coffee cup and sorted through her mail throwing away the junk and setting aside the memos and other mail that needed to be read. After a few minutes, she turned on her e-mail to send a quick reply in response to a memo asking for teachers to sign up for a dish to share at the end of the year picnic. Once she sent this, she began to open each new e-mail and respond. As the bell rang for homeroom to begin, her coffee had grown cold and she still had two e-mails to go.

Students began to filter in and the late bell rang just as the last student slid into his desk. Martha Beth quickly glanced at the room to establish attendance and sent the roster in, which was done digitally requiring Martha Beth to minimize her e-mail before sending. Once the announcements came on, Martha Beth returned to her e-mail, finishing just in time to wish the students a good day and pass out the flyer about prom. As the students exited, she glanced at the clock. Three minutes to get to the ladies room and back to write up the agenda before first period.

It was no surprise that Martha Beth spent the remainder of the day one step behind. Her classes went well and she enjoyed working with the students, but she always felt rushed. Luckily this morning, it was only the e-mail that kept her behind, other days it was chatting in the office about the newest policy, finishing a photocopy for the day, talking with a student about a problem, or even responding to memos. Martha Beth liked to stay up on her paperwork and take care of things as they immediately came to her attention.

Right before last period, she was called to the office to pick up a package. When she got there, the secretary was deep in conversation with the history teacher, Marc, a longtime friend of Martha Beth's. Hesitant to interrupt, Martha Beth held back for a moment.

"Excuse me." She paused. "I got a call to come down and pick up something." Martha Beth smiled apologetically for intruding on the conversation.

"Oh, no problem. Now, where did I put that?" The secretary turned and moved some items around on the desk. "Hmm, I can't seem to find it anywhere. I'll have to get back to you on that." She laughed a bit and shook her head in confusion.

"Hey, Martha Beth, let me walk back to class with you." Marc smiled and nodded at the secretary.

"Sure, but I have to run. I've got a class coming in." Martha Beth had a senior class on their way into the room.

The two teachers briskly walked side by side to class chatting and then turned toward her door. Rather than continue on his way, Marc stepped behind Martha Beth to enter the room. She didn't even have time to consider why when a call came out beyond the open door.

"Surprise!" Her senior students called out with cheer and Martha Beth had to stop a moment in the door to take in what they had done in the few minutes she was gone from the room. The desks were pushed together and a cake was center stage. A banner hung from the white board declaring, "Happy Birthday." She heard Marc laughing behind her.

"Were you in on this?" Martha Beth asked, turning to Marc.

"We had to get you out of the room somehow" he declared. "Go in, go in." Both teachers stepped into the room enjoying the fun.

The students had been planning this for a week once they found out it was to be Martha Beth's thirty-second birthday. Momentarily considering her lesson plan and then dismissing it in favor of enjoying the moment with her students, Martha Beth cut a second piece of cake. Shakespeare would have to wait; you only get a thirty-second birthday cake with your students once.

Review

One of Martha Beth's major problems is that she is incapable of deciding what is important to do first. She cannot discern between urgent tasks that must be attended to right away and other less time-sensitive and important tasks. For Martha Beth, everything is important, and she begins to waste energy and time on what can wait. In her mind, she prioritizes and believes that by going through each item of mail in her mailbox (both in paper and digital form) and responding, she is saving a paper shuffle for later. She tries to attend to each potential call for her attention each day, and while others may appreciate this, it is pulling her in many directions at once.

Finally, during her last class period, Martha Beth is able to weigh the events and decide that to enjoy the moment with her students is more important than the immediate attention to the lesson she had planned. To decide this is a deliberate, conscious choice and one that she needs to make more often in less obvious situations.

For Martha Beth, and most other teachers, the need to be validated in one's work is important. The students have reciprocated in care by displaying their appreciation of Martha Beth in the party. They went out of their way to purchase a banner, make a cake, and coax the history teacher in on the surprise. This event will prove to be a stress reduction for Martha Beth if she is able to successfully live in the moment and not worry about keeping on schedule with the lesson, the e-mails yet to be answered, the grades yet to be averaged, and the pot roast at home in the crock pot. When unexpected events occur, especially pleasant ones, we need to allow them the space to play out rather than rigidly sticking to our routine. A flat tire on the way to work must be repaired as time permits and no amount of worry can make it magically appear so you can be to work on time. That's why cell phones were invented! Problem solve to the best of your ability and move on: don't let the event manage you—you manage the event and you decide what is urgent and needs your attention first. Keep in mind, often tasks feel urgent, but are not important and can be moved aside for more pressing matters. For instance, not every e-mail needs to be attended to right away.

Consider This

Take a look at your day and examine the tasks that take up your time throughout. Are there tasks that you expend a disproportionate amount of time on that are not urgent or important but feel as if they require your immediate attention? Helping to break up a fist fight in the hallway is both urgent and important, answering the e-mail about what dish to bring to the year-end picnic is neither! Begin to frame these events better for yourself and question if they really require your immediate attention. Is an impromptu birthday celebration as important as devoting a full class period to Shakespeare's use of the double entendre? Is it as urgent? Who will be impacted by the decision? Clearly, Martha Beth decides that spending a few minutes on cake and pushing the lesson to the second half of the class is more beneficial. Others may not agree and might require students to get their cake and return to their desks to begin the lesson; still others may ask that the cake be put away entirely. Martha Beth attends to not only her needs to enjoy the validation of her work and later return to the lesson, but also the needs of her students in letting them know that their efforts are appreciated and meaningful.

As teachers, we often devote a large portion of our time to responding to unimportant and routine tasks. We also have a large number of routine tasks that are important (such as completing midterm grades). In responding to all of our life's tasks, we cannot forget those that will replenish and nourish our teaching selves in order that we can continue with the other mundane, routine, and often unimportant tasks that we have framed as urgent. I often feel a sense of urgency in grading my students' papers to return them as soon as possible. Recently, a friend pointed out to me that one class day won't make a huge difference, and yes, I should give myself permission to enjoy the one warm day in March to take my three-year-old daughter outside to play. We should not need to rely on others with an outside perspective to point this out to us. We need to be present in our lives and take up those moments that will most nurture ourselves. At the same time, what will most nourish and nurture our students? Will yet another vocabulary quiz, test preparation day, or essay response? In planning our curriculum, often what we would find most rewarding and nourishing intellectually and emotionally is not what we have come to expect as "school work." If we enjoy our work and find it rewarding, our stress levels will decrease and we will be much more effective in the classroom and in the school community.

CAROL—ELEMENTARY SCHOOL TEACHER IN AN INCLUSION CLASSROOM

Carol enjoys her work with her third grade students and takes joy in observing the gains students make every day. She also appreciates the interaction between the students of various ability ranges within her inclusion classroom. Recently, however, she has had personal conflict with one of the push-in teaching assistants and the animosity hovering under the surface is impacting her ability to manage her stress. At the end of the day, she finds that she is exhausted and has little energy left to continue to create engaging lessons. In a rut, Carol is frustrated and fears it will impact the students and undo the excellent progress she has made this year. In addition, Carol has the added pressure of the state tests in English and math in the coming month and she fears that the students are not yet ready.

Case Study Vignette

Carol crossed the room to the literacy corner to check on the small group of students who were starting the station on the theme for the day. Her long skirt moved about her legs freely and she lifted her face up to the sun streaming in the large windows in the back of the room. She paused in her steps for just a moment to enjoy the sun and the quiet chatter of the students engaged in their centers.

"Give it back," the unmistakable shrill voice of Claire, a sensitive child, prone to tantrums, rang through the room. Carol redirected her gaze to see Claire reaching wildly for an object the teaching assistant, Dean, had in his hand.

"No, I already told you to put it away twice. Now, sit quietly and this may come back to you at the end of the day." Dean, a push-in teaching assistant who joined Carol's class every afternoon, spoke in a stern, crisp voice. His large voice tended to carry across the room and by this point all eyes were on Claire and Dean. None of the other students were on task.

Carol turned to the literacy group, "I'll be right back, keep going." Moving around obstacles, Carol made her way to Dean in just a matter of seconds. By now, Claire was crying and throwing crayons about the room. Carol knelt beside Claire's small body seated at the round table and began to speak softly to her. At the same time, she reached up her hand to Dean expecting him to place the object in her hand. Without even looking at it, Carol knew what it was. Every day for the past two weeks, Claire brought to class with her a small soft blue train. It was small enough to hide inside an adult hand and was intended to top a pencil. Claire's newest comfort object was acquired after a recent pleasure train ride with her family. Often, students had comfort objects or comfort items of clothing and by third grade most could be separated from their objects during the school day or had lost the need to have the item at all during the day. Claire however needed her item. Throughout the school year, the items had changed, but they were always small and usually soft. Typically, letting her have the items was not a problem, but Dean saw them as a distraction.

With her hand still in the air, Carol turned to look at Dean. He made no move to place the item in her hand.

"I told her she could have it at the end of the day. She was not working on her handout; instead she was driving that train on the lines of the paper like it was a track." Dean stood in a confrontational posture.

"Thank you for helping, but if you could give it to me now and then check on the literacy group that would be great." Carol made no attempt to rise and still stayed next to Claire, careful not to lean into the young girl's personal space or touch her as often this would make a tantrum worse. Dean thrust the train at Carol, shot her a dark look, and moved toward the back of the room to join the literacy group. Along the way, he felt it necessary to reprimand two other children for not focusing on their work.

Claire still crying and her face blotchy and red refused to look at Carol. Carol quietly placed the train at the top of the handout and then spent the next few minutes drawing Claire back out and attempting to engage her in the handout. Eventually, Claire set back to work with the train tightly held in her hand.

The rest of the afternoon passed and Dean stepped out before the final dismissal bell so Carol had no chance to speak with him about the day or the incident with Claire. Lately, Carol wondered how to go about trying to resolve this disagreement in teaching practices with Dean and once again the chance to talk to him was lost. It wouldn't be until later that evening when she would finally relax again and feel as she did that moment when the sun hit her face in the classroom—and be at ease.

Review

Carol enjoys her work and the children, but she is at odds with Dean, her teaching assistant. Dean is resistant to Carol's attempts to talk and brings a sense of antagonism into the classroom, directed not only at Carol, but at the children as well. Carol is hesitant to bring in administration to resolve the differences with Dean and prefers to handle problems in her own classroom.

Unfortunately, the problems with Dean impact not only how Carol reacts to him and manifests side effects of stress such as tense muscles and slight insomnia, but he also has a negative impact on the students and the sense of community in the classroom. In addition, it is affecting her energy levels and her ability to plan. With state tests looming ahead, Carol has a hard time balancing stress, which in another school year would be routine.

Clearly, a primary concern for Carol is her interactions with Dean and his interactions with the students. This is not a situation that should be put off and will continue to worsen until it comes to a crisis point. By the time a stress instigator reaches a crisis point, it is usually destructive and difficult to resolve. Carol should attempt to talk with Dean as early as possible in order to prevent crisis. If the problem is left to worsen, Dean and Carol may begin to resent each other and the work of teaching.

Waiting until a crisis point is not beneficial in any situation. Often, individuals hope the problem will resolve without intervention. Problems do not go away; they only evolve into other problems. In the case of Dean and Carol, letting the problem fester has only made it more difficult a conversation to broach. Dean, perhaps feeling hostility from and/or toward Carol, leaves the room early to avoid interactions with her.

Although Carol does not like the idea of bringing anyone else into the problem, a conflict resolution meeting with a mediator may be a good idea. This person does not need to be an administrator. An open and honest dialogue may bring about some surprising connections. For instance, perhaps Dean feels attacked by Carol or perhaps he feels as if he is undermined in the classroom. Carol may discover that it isn't Dean she has a problem with, but in reality, she is opposed to "intruders" in her classroom. The goal of this dialogue would be to air grievances and to create a goal strategy plan that will enable the coworkers to find common ground and set expectations clearly.

At some point, even the easiest going of individuals may find themselves at the center of conflict and it is important not to ignore the situation. Communication is instrumental in resolving issues of this nature, and without this dialogue, both parties will continue to develop stress and the situation will worsen. Once one is already stressed, the ability to deal with conflict is also impacted and one often does not respond appropriately. It is also very important for Carol and Dean to resolve their differences because they are a model for the young students in the classroom and young people are very astute. Carol may feel she is hiding her antagonism toward Dean, but the young people in the room probably are very aware of the situation.

When seeking resolution to conflict, it is also important to remember that resolution is not about being "right." Dean and Carol need to work together to create an agreement that will work for both of them in order to move forward. The focus of the conversation should not be about placing blame or assigning guilt.

It is also not a conversation that can be carried through e-mail. I often hear of young people who attempt to resolve workplace conflict through e-mail or another digital means. The problem here is the lack of face-to-face communication and also that often our words are misconstrued through e-mail. Meeting face-to-face allows for immediate communication and clarity of thoughts.

Carol could perhaps let Dean know that she would like him to stay late to chat. Perhaps he has a legitimate need to leave early such as picking up his daughter after school. In which case, Carol should not expect him to stay that day, but could offer to meet him the next day if need be or at another time, such as earlier before classes begin. She should also give him a reason for meeting, such as a need to "discuss how we work together and planning." This allows Dean to see that there is a set topic and that it will be a team effort and not an attack. It also allows him to plan some responses.

In addition, just the act of taking steps to help resolve a conflict can be beneficial. It may be a small step forward, but at least the individual is pulling away from the mire that has created stress.

Consider This

Take a look at the people you interact with every day at school. Is there a person you have encountered difficulties working with at the school? Is this situation creating a negative working environment leading to stress? If so, have you talked with the person or is this a dialogue you are putting off in hopes that the problem will just cure itself?

If you have identified a person you are currently in conflict with at work, sit down and do an examination of your interactions with this person to try and discover the true reason for the conflict. Often the source of conflict is not at the surface of your encounters with the individual. Carol, for instance, may have a larger issue with a sense of intrusion when push-in teachers enter her classroom. Other difficulties may be the result of miscommunication, resentment, differences in pedagogy, or personality. Often, a little introspection may help resolve a situation before it comes to a crisis point.

Look back on your journal entries and note when you recorded a sense of stress. Who were you interacting with just prior to the sensation of stress?

Sometimes we do not recognize on a conscious level when a conflict with someone is in the early stages. A slight irritation today may evolve in a crisis later unless we deal with the disruption. In speaking with teachers, I found that often this is a personality clash, and because teachers felt that it was an inappropriate reaction to be irritated, they tried to ignore or dismiss the concern. Ignoring the concern might help in the short term, but if you will be working with this individual every day for a school year or longer, as Carol is with Dean, ignoring the problem today will have a lasting effect later.

4

Revive Yourself

After reading through the stress management techniques and the case studies, review your own experiences. Hopefully, you have begun to keep a stress journal that you can review to help you identify your stress triggers and responses. Now it is time to begin to develop your plan to respond to stress. You should develop your self-care techniques before a crisis or stress event. Much like parachuting from a plane, you don't want to wait until you are in the air falling before you learn how to pull the cord. Identifying your stress triggers and responses before an event can help you know when and how to respond with a management technique. Planning ahead which technique to use can allow you to respond faster with the most suitable and effective technique. Your self-care routine should consider not only the physical self, but also the psychological, spiritual, emotional, and professional self. A balanced plan is attentive to all of the aspects of self.

Begin by examining your journal for day-to-day events, then move to more specific elements such as your work to life balance, your understanding of what is urgent and important, and your current responses to stress (unhealthy vs. healthy). Use the checklist below to guide your reflections, which you can respond to in your journal. Be sure to answer honestly. Perhaps, flipping through your journal to look for examples and connections to each item will be helpful.

STRESS MANAGEMENT CHECKLIST

1. *Balance your work and home lives.* How would you rate your work to life balance? Can it be improved? Where do you spend the bulk of your out of school time? Is your time out of the school day balanced? Do you have a sense of accomplishment and satisfaction from both your work and your out of school life? Do you allow yourself down time to engage in activities that you find to be pleasurable?

2. *Support team.* Is there someone in your life at home or at work with whom you have a positive and nourishing relationship? Can you share your day with this person and expect to have an active and constructive conversation? Is this relationship reciprocal—do you respond in an active and constructive way to the other person? Do you share both positive and negative events and do you respond to each other in healthy ways?

3. *Personal outlook.* Do you have a personal outlook and mind-set that assumes you will be successful in the classroom and school environment? Examine your own thought habits for a positive or negative pattern. Negative patterns include a critical mind-set, a wary demeanor, expectations for trouble, a sense of failure, and a focus on inadequacies and what is wrong. A positive pattern would allow the individual to feel appreciative and effective in one's work and life. Positive pattern individuals expect good outcomes, supportive relationships, know when they have success, and value all experiences. Positive individuals also focus on what is beneficial in the situation or what can be good. These individuals participate in appraisal thinking strategies and attempt to turn negatives into positives by reframing problems. Also, consider your support team, as these individuals should also be positive pattern people.

4. *Transitional zone.* Do you employ transitional zones to separate your work life from your out of school life? If so, do these zones include your support team and are they healthy transitional spaces? Do you have a variety of transitional spaces that you can put in place depending on the day?

5. *Determining levels of need and efficiency.* Examine the task. Is it urgent? Is it important? Are you placing priorities where they don't belong, thus robbing yourself of nourishing activities? Where are you focusing your attention? Examine your efficiency—what is taking longer than needed? What are you committing more time to than needed (unnecessary time for expected results)? Are you leaving time to replenish yourself?

6. *Problem solving.* Do you focus your energies on problems that can actually be solved or do you fixate on what cannot be changed? When problem solving, do you consider reframing the concern in order to examine it from other angles to provide new possible solutions?

7. *Mental preparation.* Do you prepare yourself for what you may know will be a stressful event and do you present yourself with opportunities to alleviate stress during the event? Do you foresee what may be stressful and find ways to prevent the occurrence such as through the use of time management and planning ahead?

8. *Healthy/unhealthy response.* Evaluate your responses to stressful reactions. Are these responses healthy, such as walking, exercising, talking with a supportive and active constructive individual or are they unhealthy and negative responses such as smoking or engaging in avoidance techniques like watching television?

Once you have examined specific points of your life, including stress triggers, stress reactions, and your responses to those stress reactions, you can begin to put a plan into place. You can use the worksheets included in figures 4.1 and 4.2 to plan your self-care techniques.

Other helpful stress reduction strategies can include adding the use of rituals to your day to reduce stress. Knowing the importance of a positive outlook, one can infuse the strategy of daily gratitudes. This can be done in a journal or just silently. The important aspect is in recognizing what we are grateful for in order to focus on the positive. With the goal of being a more positive person who is healthier and happier, these gratitudes can be built in as a daily ritual and incorporated into an already routine part of your day such as when showering or commuting to work. Preferably, one would do this activity at the same time every day to establish the ritual nature of the task. Think of at least three things you are grateful for every day. Some of these can be recurring gratitudes, such as thanks for your health, but try to make at least one specific to the current events in your life. For instance, I am grateful for my family, my health, and today in particular, the support of others so I can write.

Our emotions and emotional reactions to stress can be controlled. We do not have to allow stressful events to run our lives. We need to remember that our emotions are not something that happen to us, but instead are reactions

My Self-Care Techniques and Stress Response Plan

For everyday and routine stress

My Active and Constructive Support Team Includes:

My Built-in Transition Zones Include:

FIGURE 4.1

to events and as such can be controlled. Much like doing one's gratitudes, the emotional response we automatically call up based on an event is a routine. In some cases, this is a routine that must be broken. For instance, if my automatic reaction whenever I become stuck in traffic is anger, I must actively change the emotional response enough times for it to become a habit. I need to return to my self-care plan and add "stuck in traffic and anger" to my list. My self-care technique can be a cleansing breath and self-talk to calm down and alter my reaction. This will need to be consistently done multiple times before it becomes a habit (anywhere between twenty and thirty times). I will not have an instant solution or an instant routine response simply by willing it to be so; I must replace one habitual emotional response with another.

Sometimes a physical reminder is needed so that in the moment we remember the habit-changing behavior. In the car for instance, one could place a Post-it note on the dash as a reminder not to get angry in traffic. A focal

My Most Typical Stress Reactions and Self-Care Responses	
For example, pain in shoulder	*Self-talk to drop shoulders and place hands in lap for a moment of silent meditation to recenter*

My Most Typical Stress Triggers and Self-Care Management Plan	
For example, grading at the end of the semester	*Plan ahead and get a digital grading program to keep a running tally of scores*

FIGURE 4.2

point image such as the note or other visual can be used in any stress connected environment. Think about placing visual cues in places where you experience stress; you could tape a visual in the classroom above the whiteboard or chalkboard, or put a sticker on your laptop or grading book.

We must also cultivate the emotional responses to our work. Teaching is an emotional labor. We care about our students and we bring our emotional sense of being to the work based on all of the sociocultural baggage that attends teaching, such as our own experiences as a student and the media portrayals of teachers. Often, young early career teachers are identified as being full of energy and enthusiasm. This energy and enthusiasm needs to be cultivated in established and practiced teachers as well. We often start the school year off with a sense of renewal, but quickly lose it over the course of routine and by week two, old habits have returned.

In order to cultivate and retain this sense of renewal, we need to actively seek it out in our work and remember what brought us to the profession, what rewards us and validates our work, and simply, what makes us happy. Seek out opportunities to reciprocate care for other teachers within the building and help develop a sense of community to protect this commitment to reclaiming the emotional aspect of the work. Document moments in your teaching day when you are successful and hold that moment in your mind. Consider how that moment can be reclaimed again another day. Perhaps the moment is a particular teaching activity that went really well or a day when you were able to organize the entire lesson for the next day before leaving, so you felt accomplished. Those moments need to resurface again, but will require some effort on your part to allow the opportunity to do so. At the same time, consider when you are unsuccessful and prevent the circumstances that allowed that moment to occur.

Nancy Mack[1] recommends that we retain this energy and enthusiasm by identifying when we are happy, continuing to learn from our students, cherishing our literacy, finding the courage to develop new ideas, finding joy in what our students accomplish, seeking other activities beyond school to provide energy, finding ways to gather positive attitudes, claiming our own mentors, and actively deciding to think, feel, and act differently. Altering our sense of who we think we are in the classroom can help replenish our energies and allow us to reclaim that sense of anything is possible that young teachers often have. When the work becomes routine and we go to school to just do a job, we open ourselves up to stress and begin to see our work as not having value. Teachers need to have this energy and enthusiasm to be effective and to continue to do the good work they set out to do when starting a career.

NOTE

1. Nancy Mack, "Energy and Enthusiasm: Don't Start the School Year without Them," *English Journal* 98, no. 1 (2008): 18–25.

Continuing to Care: Nourish Yourself and Your Classroom

It is important to remember to care for ourselves in order to have a healthy teaching career and a healthy classroom. Much of stress management is preventative maintenance. We can nourish ourselves and our classroom environments in many ways. As you read through the following examples, consider which you already do and which you can include or try out to enrich your teaching self. Below are fifteen ways I continue to nourish myself as well as ways that teachers across my state have nourished their teaching selves.

1. *Create beauty and order in your classroom.* I can't think in disorder and neither could many of my students. In order to have a classroom that fostered a community of learners, I insisted on bringing beauty into the room in the form of student artwork on the walls and a mural painted on one wall. Not only did this make the room more attractive, it made the room feel more inviting and as it was student-produced work, students could take ownership in the space. Lucille Ogden, teacher, advocates hanging your own small child's artwork around the classroom or on the door, as it will remind students of their younger, imaginative life and may inspire their imagination to resurface.

I also insisted on a clean room. There were no collected stacks of papers left about to clutter the space. My own work space was neat and orderly. This allowed me to think clearly and added to the inviting feel of the room. Not all teachers are by nature organized and some of my fellow teachers had rooms that looked as if a tornado had hit. This is not a pleasant environment and is not productive for learning. Keep in mind that there is a balance between organized and sterile. You don't want to go to the extreme where the room feels like a hospital in the absence of personality in hopes of keeping organized.

The sounds of the classroom can also help create a positive and uplifting environment. I love a busy classroom with lots of productive noise and academic learning chatter. Some teachers prefer a quieter room, but whichever you prefer, allow yourself to accept that setting. You should avoid doing what you think a model classroom looks and sounds like because it will be inauthentic and cumbersome for your teaching. Melissa Wadsworth-Miller, middle school teacher, likes to bring music to her classroom and accomplishes this by bringing in CDs or her iPod to school. She plays music while grading, while students are working, or when she has kids in after school for help. It lightens both her mood and theirs, and it helps her bond with the middle school students.

2. *Welcome the day and your class.* I always like to greet my classes, and when teaching high school, I stood at the door to welcome students to the room. Even now, I often greet each student as he or she enters the room and welcome students who arrive before me. I want my students to know that this is a friendly space and one that cultivates academic relationships between instructor and student. It helps set the tone for the class. As Lucille Ogden, teacher, puts it, "No computer work or desk work is more important than those first minutes of the teaching day when your students arrive."

3. *Bring a sense of nature and life to your work spaces.* I really believe that it is important to bring a sense of nature to your work spaces to keep connected. This was very difficult for me to do in my first teaching classroom as I had no windows. I had to keep rotating plants in that were still alive! I currently keep plants in both my home office and my work office to continue this use of living plants as a way to stay connected to the outdoors. This also helps create an inviting space for students. I know other teachers who keep a goldfish or other small animal in their classes as well.

4. *Teach what matters.* I realize that we have state as well as national content standards. We have content that must be instructed, but we also have some choice in other aspects of the content we introduce and how we choose to introduce that content. As an English teacher, I did not think of my curriculum as a series of novels, or a listing of literary terms, although we certainly did cover those materials. Instead, I defined my curriculum by essential ques-

tions and what I wanted students to learn about life and the world around them. We need to teach what matters and we need to teach students to think independently. I believe that the mark of a good teacher is one who is able to help students to the point where they only need the teacher for guidance because the inquiry and search for answers is completed independently by the students. This will nourish you and the students.

5. *Allow yourself to accept compliments.* I admit, I have had a hard time with this one. We are so quick to find fault with our own work that we often do not see the great gains we make with our students. Many of us also tend to dismiss compliments by saying, "oh, it was nothing." Learn from those compliments and value yourself as much as others (if not more than others) do. Whether it be a good lesson, a class project, or your volunteer work to help organize senior graduation, accept the compliments and use them to help validate your work.

6. *Thank yourself.* We also have to remember to thank ourselves and compliment ourselves. We know when we have a good class session and we see each time we go out of our way to help a student. Rather than allow these moments to just pass by as part of our job description, we need to slow down and thank ourselves for the success or for the help we give others. Like accepting compliments, this will help us validate our work and help us to appreciate all we do.

7. *Form a collaborative study team.* This idea comes from Janet Gallant, an English Language Arts coach and elementary school principal. Janet provides a copy of a very brief article from a professional journal to those who have signed up to discuss that particular topic. Teachers and paraprofessionals have a few days to read the article and perhaps try the new strategy or idea in their classroom. The group then meets together in the conference room to talk about the ideas presented in the article. The energy in a room full of dedicated teachers discussing classroom instruction and student learning is a wonderful source of nourishment. Janet also points out that so is the coffee and fresh muffins that she always serves at these morning gatherings.

Often, teacher centers will help sponsor a collaborative learning group and will pay for reading materials and other costs associated with organizing the group. At my current job, we often get together for brown bag lunches to collaborate and talk about projects that are in progress. Sharing not only helps develop a community of teachers, but can also provide new ideas for projects. Teacher Rick Kugler participates in a healthy version of the collaborative group with a salad day. A small group of his colleagues agreed to spend one day each week making a salad together. They e-mailed the assigned ingredients a week ahead or decided together at that week's meal what each one would bring the following week. The salads were tasty, the conversation fun, and participants felt a sense of community each time. Cathy Holbrook, teacher, also advocates for lunch with colleagues and believes that it is important to "resist the temptation to squeeze in a little grading, but instead just sit, eat, and decompress. It is a great way to get fresh input for all kinds of things: teaching ideas especially, but also discipline, tough parents, and so on."

8. *Share our work.* This idea from Victor Jaccarino, administrator, reminds us to share our successful lessons, methods, and experiences. He also advocates for "stealing" ideas. Borrowing ideas from each other allows us to develop our collection of what I like to call "teacher toolbox" methods. Without a rich and diverse toolbox, we tend to rely on the same methods and teaching techniques unit after unit. We should share to continue to learn new ideas. This can occur within our own schools or at the many professional development activities that are available. For example, every year I attend my state teaching conference for my content area. Often I present, but I always attend as many sessions as possible. I find that the experience rejuvenates me and fuels me with lots of great ideas to carry back to my school.

9. *Create a reading environment.* Paul O'Brien, English teacher, has two rocking chairs on an old Oriental rug in his classroom. Framing two sides of this setting are two bookcases. Often he finds himself sitting in a chair chatting with a student or reading a book. He also has tons of pictures of students, both past and present, creating a kind of student history and puts up newspaper articles about students, from sports events to mock trial victories. This creates a personal space for students to enjoy relaxing and reading. Students become invested in the space as it is for them and dedicated to them. In my own classroom, I always had a rug and couch by my free read bookshelf. I also found that indirect lighting was beneficial to setting the stage for this space and included a lava lamp and side table lamp. Students often gravitated to this space in free time and when working on silent reading or individual projects. Lucille Ogden, teacher, also advocates for at least once a marking period sending around a list of what students are reading and then posting it in the room and encouraging the chatter before class to be about books. We should also

share what we are reading. Students learn to appreciate the lifelong positive habit of reading by seeing others model the behavior both at home and at school. We should nourish our literate selves as well and the belief that reading can be relaxing and pleasant.

10. *Lighten the commute.* Another suggestion from teacher Rick Kugler is to have a more enjoyable commute. He suggests listening to books on tape or listening to relaxing music. I also listen to books on tape and have found that if I attend local publishing house year-end clearance sales, I can get books on CD for a really great price. At my public library there is a huge collection as well, so I need to purchase few books. Having had an hour commute, I know the importance of making this time relaxing. Without creating a pleasant atmosphere, the traffic (or in winter months, the road conditions) can create an appetizer of stress before I even get to work. By lifting the mood in the car, I am better prepared to meet the challenges of the day. On the way home, this is a great place to create a transition zone. I listen to my MP3 player and have a song list that is uplifting. After adding a baby to my commute, I had to find a way to make the ride more pleasant for both of us as I drop her off at day care while I teach. Now, my toddler and I sing along to Laurie Berkner (one musical artist we can agree on!) or we play I spy games. Believe me when I say a cranky toddler in the car on the way to work makes for a cranky day.

11. *Learn how to say no.* Often, we as teachers join many committees and get involved with other activities beyond our teaching day. Susan Kitson, teacher, points out that we need to learn to say no firmly and without regret and recommends that it helps if you cannot say no right out, to say, "Please let me think about that and I will get back to you." That way you have time to remind yourself that you really don't have time for another yes. I have found that I suffer from this problem and get involved in multiple committees and special projects at a time. Often I find it hard to just sit back on a committee and do a simple task and before long I am directing the project. We need to have a clear look at our scheduling and have a realistic understanding of how much we can do in one day without becoming stressed. Susan also points out that you need to be selective in the projects you become involved with and learn how to participate in those that nourish you over those that will only cause stress. For instance, I always found that working with the drama students and helping to put on an annual play was very rewarding. It was stressful, but it was a good stress and I loved the end result every year. Other

projects end up feeling like an act of futility and I regret adding it to my already packed schedule.

12. *Connect the many parts of your world.* Maureen Glessing-Senska, teacher, has a spiritual and physical nourishment routine that includes going into the woods every day after school to decompress and be with nature. She also does yoga in the morning and with her advisory students. She says, "I teach them to deep breathe—I surround myself with positive people and steer clear of negative ones. . . . I try to learn something new or stretch myself with some new learning as often as possible. I push myself to look at things from multiple perspectives, particularly from the marginalized viewpoint—either through reading or through my social circle. . . . When I need to, I go for a massage!" This fantastic plan for nourishing the teaching self connects nature to the classroom, students to teacher, and the physical to the spiritual. In all ways, Maureen connects the many parts of her world.

13. *Allow yourself to be tired.* This advice comes from Susan Kitson, teacher, and she notes that we must get the rest we need. "I always feel that the amount of energy I have to teach is my first gift to my students, I try not to over-do." Not only is it important to rest when you are tired, but also when your body is ill or run down. In my early career, I often went to school ill just because I didn't want to take a sick day. Of course, in my belief, I was displaying how hard I could work, but I was also exposing others to germs—not good. Once after having four impacted wisdom teeth removed the day before, I attempted to go to work. Luckily for me, my principal realized how much pain I was in and sent me home. Much like our "frontier" attitude that keeps us isolated from each other, it has also given us an unbalanced view of what a hard work ethic is. It is not beneficial for anyone to attend work ill or in pain. We need to learn to take time for ourselves when needed. If we don't, not only can we suffer, but those around us will as well. Susan points out that not only do we need to stay well and healthy for ourselves and our work, but more important, for our families, who need us as well.

14. *Stay fit.* Also in connection with staying healthy and knowing your limits, the need to exercise and stay hydrated is important. Lucille Ogden, teacher, listed "drinking water" as one of the top three ways she stays nourished in her teaching self. As we work throughout our day, we often forget to stay hydrated. A cup of coffee and whatever I drank at lunch, usually soda, was not a good way to stay hydrated. Often, I find that my own students as

they begin student teaching forget their own health and resort to poor eating habits and forget to exercise. In order to reduce our stress loads and nourish ourselves, we must remember to stay fit and care for our bodies—you only get one! I freeze a water bottle at night and take it with me every day. This way I have access to cold spring water throughout the day.

15. *Smile.* A positive attitude can do much for nourishing yourself and helping you see the possibilities in every day.

6

Find Your Niche of Caring and Honor Your Work

English professor Stephanie Paterson writes about her teaching life as a fast-moving river. "I can never stop the flow of the river. I can, however, stop midstream and stand on a boulder pausing to take in the sunlight."[1] These midstream pauses are an excellent metaphor for what I advocate in this book. Pause and reflect. Take in the power of your work, remind yourself why it is worth it, but also take stock about what isn't working. Refuse to accept a Band-Aid approach to long-term stress, or a philosophy in which if you ignore it—maybe it will go away. While midstream, look at those passing beside you and reach out to help others as well. This reciprocal care will help foster a community of caring.

I encourage you to create a stress management team, wellness team, or community of caring group in your own school. With the right support, we can enable our school communities to be more stress free and more about caring. Encouraging nurturing behaviors and assisting those teachers who already do this work could begin in teacher education programs and through professional development within the schools. Over time, these approaches, which might initially encounter resistance, would begin to change. Good teaching is more than method, technique, and a good classroom management plan. It is also about the "*connective* capacity"[2] between students and teachers as well as between teachers to each other and students to each other. This connection is the basis for compassion and nurturing in teaching, but with it comes the risk of opening oneself emotionally.

Ana from the narrative case study in chapter 3 was lucky to have a background in counseling, which allowed her to have additional techniques for dealing with student emotional needs and the resultant stress that occurs for teachers from being emotionally connected to students. Most teachers do not have this background and it is an aspect that could easily be added to teacher education programs. Teacher education programs are already packed with courses on literacy, management, educational psychology, and adolescent development, but addressing a teacher's needs are not typically attended to in these programs. At most, students may have a seminar that is offered concurrently with student teaching and stress might be a short talk one day during the seminar amid all the other concerns that must be addressed during this crucial time in one's training.

A model for this type of course already exists and is part of the instruction at the University of California, San Francisco, School of Medicine. Here, individuals in medical training participate in a course called "The Healer's Art," which focuses on compassion and the aspect of human wholeness. Students explore how to interact with others (patients) while also attending to their own wholeness and ability to connect with the emotional needs of the self. According to Remen, every social interaction reinforces the "wounds of the cultural shadow" and that it is "very difficult for an individual to heal alone."[3] The course teaches students exercises in emotional healing and if applied to teaching would promote the act of teachers helping teachers while doing the work of attending to the nurturing and emotional needs of their students.

The activities that are learned in the teacher preparation course could also be communicated through professional development activities for those teachers already in the field. Teachers could participate in activities encouraged by the administration or better yet organized by peer teachers in order to promote nurturing and care of the self. Teachers could be encouraged to do what Remen calls "unload[ing] the baggage."[4] Teachers could also organize a type of problem-solving support group in which they recognize the needs of students, attempt to help find solutions, and then also allow room for teachers to grieve the students they have "lost," those students for instance who they were not able to connect with in time to keep from dropping out of school.

These approaches to nurturing and compassion should not be limited to the role of the teacher, but should become part of the student's experience in school as well. In discussing holistic education, Miller points out that modern schooling does not serve the spiritual unfoldment of the child. It serves capitalism, nationalism and a reductionist worldview. It serves a society that is completely committed to meritocracy, where there's fierce competition between individuals to reach the top of a social hierarchy.[5]

The student from a very early age could be encouraged to support other students rather than focus on competition and the "frontier values" identified by Remen. Nel Noddings (1994) suggests that dialogue is the key to this wholeness approach to students and teaching. In her article, "An Ethic of Caring and Its Implications for Instructional Arrangements," Noddings encourages open dialogue and calls for time to be granted for such activities. Time is essential as "teacher and student must know each other well enough for trust to develop."[6] Students in turn would have opportunities to practice caring and would take those lessons with them through their education and into adulthood. As Noddings states, "The caring teacher also wants students to have practice in caring."[7]

One problem is that stress has become commonplace and is accepted as part of the job rather than as something that is a problem to be resolved. Another concern is that the term *stress* has become overused and is often applied to less severe situations in which the individual is simply a little worried or tense.

Stress cannot be targeted as a problem within one population or school environment. It can't even be tied to a simple division between experienced or fledgling teachers. Stress affects all populations regardless of age or the socioeconomic status of the community and school, regardless of the type of school, and regardless of one's pedagogy. It is also a timeless issue. Stress is not dependent on a testing culture (although that doesn't help), students engaging in technology and disengaging from the classroom, or the cry that students are less motivated. There are many stressors that really have little to do with actual classroom teaching and more to do with school politics, auxiliary paperwork, and school violence. What we are missing in schools is community and a sense of belonging, not only to the school, but to each other.

In my time in an alternative high school, I quickly learned how to manage simple stressors, and despite my best efforts, I still experienced stress throughout my career at this school. I was the most productive and managed stress the best when I was actively engaged in a community of teachers who supported each other and were supported by the administration. We also made great effort to extend this sense of community to the students in order to engage them in a larger commitment to each other, and I believe it helped benefit both the staff and the students. We need to be aware of each other and support each other. If we do not do this, then the entire school could suffer. When a teacher is stressed in third period and reacts harshly to a student, it doesn't end there. That student will carry that emotional event into fourth period and will affect that community space, which in turn will affect the next in line. This spillover effect quickly moves throughout a whole school.

Community and reciprocal care are important in educational settings. When teachers are working with students, the emotional elements of the career are bound to impact the teacher. Teachers can have many positive emotional events and can even have positive nurturance suffering emotional events in a teaching day. But in order to best do the work of teaching and keep teachers in the field, new teachers need to be prepared for what they will experience and both new and experienced teachers alike should create a management plan.

DIGITAL CARING COMMUNITIES

Sometimes, because of a number of reasons, it is difficult to structure a live face-to-face group of engaged supporters to foster a community of caring. For instance, in my student teaching seminar course, students are spread all over the state and we only meet in person a few times a semester. This makes it difficult for us to support each other in what can be a very challenging time. Students often experience a great deal of stress and because they are in new and temporary environments, they very rarely have a community of caring present within the work environment. In order to combat the stress and the simple negotiating of a new identity role, we meet digitally.

While not as gratifying as a face-to-face meeting, our digital group still operates and functions as a face-to-face meeting would, but something is always missing. It is preferable to meet in person because of the intimacy of human sharing. The facial expressions, the expression within verbal sharing, and the use of body language to comfort another person is not present when meeting online. Even a video Skype meeting carried over the Internet cannot be as effective as a face-to-face meeting. A digital world does provide other possibilities however, such as the ability to post your concern at any time, even at 3 am when you can't sleep. Responders can respond at any time and this provides an opportunity for people to reflect rather than feel the need to comment at the moment the concern is shared. It also allows for the caring community to be much larger than what one may typically find in a school setting where very often the individual shares with only one or two other people. Our student teaching digital group numbers are different every semester, but typically we average around ten people, which makes a larger more flexible group, but still small enough to be manageable.

When the student teaching group first began to "meet," we used a blog. The problem that we found with the blog is that it was very stagnate and became a call and response forum. We later met on a Ning site and found that to be much more beneficial. This social networking site for closed community members allowed for many applications to stay connected. Students liked this format as it had many similar features as Facebook, a site with which they were already very familiar. As "digital natives," these students were comfortable with an online presence for communication and sharing personal thoughts. Using our Ning network, we could stay connected in many ways, including posting pictures, notes, blogs, discussion forums, and my favorite—a live chat. Ning also allowed for individual conversations through e-mails and notes directly to the individual's page. We had a home site to share and each participant had an individual page that could be personalized depending on the individual's needs.

The first day of our seminar class we meet on campus before going to the first student teaching placement. We set up our Ning network and also read about "clearness committees" from Parker Palmer's *The Courage to Teach*.[8] These committees adopted from a Quaker structure, invite individuals to join together to sort out personal problems. The original form of these meetings is quite structured and involves many roles. Because we did not feel as a class that this form would benefit us, we altered it a bit to better meet our needs. The key to this was that students negotiated as a class how to best use Ning as our clearness committee rather than me, as the professor, dictating the process. These guidelines were posted on the front page of our Ning site. The guidelines varied from specific goals such as asking that we each check our Ning network once a week and join live chat when possible—to more of a recommendation for participants to try to end each "venting stress session" with a positive gratitude. We also took into consideration Palmer's focus person role[9] and decided that each conversation should be devoted to only one person's issues. If one student posts a discussion forum about a stressful situation, then the conversation stays focused on that one student. If students have their own concerns to bring up, they should not be shared in an existing forum, but instead should start their own. Under this guideline, multiple forums or discussions could occur simultaneously.

We had great success with our Ning network. Students checked it regularly and used it beyond my original intentions. Students used it for a wide variety of purposes, including using it to stay in contact with friends in the class, seek clarification on assignments, share funny vignettes from student teaching, and have personal contact with me. At the same time, our stress unloading, or "venting" as we came to call it, occurred in concert with the more personalized uses and students were able to support each other in a digital community of caring.

You could create a digital community with people from your own district or create one to invite people from across the state or even a wider audience to participate. Often, professional content organizations host digital sites for new teachers or for specific topics. For instance, the New York State English Council has hosted discussion sites for new teachers and teachers interested in teacher inquiry research. The National Council of Teacher of English also has similar groups and hosts in-person meetings at the annual convention.

Hopefully, you can find the right community of caring for your needs. Be it a digital community or a face-to-face community, you must find the right niche for your needs. Finding a group that is positive and not selfish may take some searching, but there is a group for everyone, even if that group is just a team of supporters who rally around you when needed and comprises only a few key people. Keep in mind as well that your group does not need to be other teachers. A similar audience may be beneficial, but sometimes the most effective care groups are those comprising people removed from the environment that causes stress.

My own community of caring includes a past college student about the same age as me and living in the same nearby town with a daughter the same age as my own, a mentor in the form of a woman who teaches similar courses at another college (and whose past position I now fill), my husband, and birth family including my mother who is also involved with education at the high school level. With these individuals, I can share my stress regarding my work and the challenges I face, including those of a nurturing nature. These individuals do not listen to my worries and attempt to offer ready solutions. Instead they listen and reflect with me. Together we either come to a solution or manage the knowledge that this is a temporary stress to be carried without resolution.

MOTHERING, NURTURING, AND ACADEMIA

When I first became pregnant, I was still teaching high school and was finishing the writing of my dissertation. I had hopes of finding a tenure track position at the college level and had started the arduous process of applying for and interviewing for positions. I had not expected to become pregnant, but after a long battle with infertility and several miscarriages, my doctor delivered the news that I was pregnant. I received this news while in the exam room with my husband, preparing to tell the doctor that I was ready to give up trying and go off the fertility medication. I also received this news just a few days after accepting a position at a four-year college over an hour's drive from our home.

In just a few months, I started teaching a full course load at the college, defended my dissertation while eight months' pregnant, and delivered a healthy baby by cesarean a few short weeks later. A few months after all that, my husband got a new job and we sold our house and bought a new house closer to work. This, believe it or not, was a bit stressful! Without my strategies to cope with stress and my community of caring, I do not think I would have made it through those experiences with my sanity intact. Much like Anjalee Deshpande Nadkarni's vignette from *Mama, PhD*,[10] I found myself in Ohio at an ethnography conference away from my young baby, but committed to my presentation and ready for a crying meltdown as I pumped milk and stored it in my hotel's mini fridge to bring home at the end of my four-day trip. Luckily, I had company on the trip and my support community was only a quick phone call away.

There is a particular vein of stress that emerges when attempting to mother for the first time and enter the world of academia. I quickly became adept at code switching and border crossing. I found I was able to with ease move from talking about "Dora the Explorer" to the academic jargon associated with teaching secondary English education and literacy courses. I could pump breast milk in my office and moments later race off to class to lecture about critical literacy and discourse. Crossing these borders did not come without a cost however, and I increasingly found that I felt guilt and stress. I felt guilt and stress any time I dropped off my daughter at day care to go to campus. I felt guilt and stress any time I was with my daughter and enjoying daily events such as bath time because I wasn't working on publication or grading papers.

I found my department chair to be incredibly supportive through all of this. I have heard horror stories of women attempting to fulfill the dual roles of mother and academic with limited success. While I too found (and still find) it to be a challenge, my support network included a supportive chair. He took over my courses while on maternity leave, scheduled me for classes that were flexible in meeting throughout the semester, such as a student teaching seminar, encouraged me to bring my daughter to meetings if I was stuck for a sitter, and even took to calling her our most junior faculty member as she often attended meet and greet events and other department events. I was fortunate to have a small cadre of professors who refused to accept a dated paradigm for the role of professor. The discourse of mother and professor merged and I was better for it.

At the same time, there were also other challenges. Anyone who has tried to write while a two-year-old repeatedly attempts to climb up and "type" and refuses to take a much needed nap, is familiar with the stress that accompanies this struggle. While I could pump breast milk in my private office, other areas of campus were not as flexible. When teaching out of my home building, I had to pump in the ladies room. While at a whole campus required training on, of all topics, diversity, I had to pump in a storage closet next to a mop and was asked by the man leading the training if I really had to leave. When traveling to visit student teachers who worked in schools over an hour and a half from my home, I pumped in my car. This was a new and unique stress. One that I had no background for how to handle and one over which, admittedly, I felt some sense of shame. In part, the shame came from being placed in the situation to start with, but on a larger scale it came from a resolute agreement with myself that I would never back down and I felt myself slipping. It came from a strong feminist background and my frustration in that I often quietly accepted the situation rather than challenged it.

As I grew as a mother, I found ways to cope with the stress that came from attempting the balancing act of mother and professor. I eventually added new members to my community of caring. These members were also mothers and individuals who could help me navigate the wobbly barrier I had established between my teaching life and personal life. They also encouraged me to break down that barrier when needed, so that for instance when my daughter's day care closed early for staff training and I had no one to watch her, she came with me to a campuswide poster session on educational strategies. I needed someone to grant me "permission" to allow these barriers to blend.

At the same time, I found myself struggling with the desire to continue the role of the nurturing teacher as I had with my high school students. I thought that having students for such a brief time would have required a different role of me, but even with college students I had for only a semester or two, I found that I played the role of nurturer. In the role of nurturer, I still worried about my students and carried that worry home. Admittedly, it was not to the level I had with my high school students, but it was still there. I worried about Sara living with a persistent mold problem in her small basement apartment; I worried about Steve getting his teaching exams taken in time to finish his program; I worried about Alison and her stress levels and her cruel host teacher. This nurturance came out of a desire for my students to have the best possible college experience and came from an honest desire to help. Occasionally, students would comment about it on my written evaluations at the end of a course and note a particular time they felt I cared about them as a person. Although this nurturance suffering was slight compared to my teaching high school experiences, I still very much relied on my community of caring to help me through, and in some ways that community grew to include the students themselves, depending on the concerns.

HONOR YOUR WORK

We experience many kinds of stress in our teaching lives and everyone has a different reaction to stresses. Some stress is positive stress and enables us to perform better at a task. Without enough positive stress, one's performance may suffer because the task is not challenging or rewarding. At the same time, people have different thresholds for stress. I, for instance, am a planner and stress kicks in early for me for any given task. If grades are due at 3 pm on Friday, I want to have them done by Wednesday, just in case anything goes wrong. My husband on the other hand is a procrastinator and does not feel stress until it is actually imperative that he complete the task. Short-term task-related stress is acceptable in our lives if we know how to plan for it and manage it day to day. It is the long-term and debilitating stress that we must seek to avoid if possible and manage through a detailed stress plan.

We need to best learn how to manage our stress in order to continue the good work that we do with our students. Not every technique will work for everyone and not every technique will work with every situation. A stress relief method that worked yesterday may not work again as well today depending on the circumstances. You should be prepared to have several options available in your preparedness plan and decide which technique from your arsenal you think will work best at the moment. Consult your community of caring by whatever name you call it and wherever it appears and seek out an ear (or eyes on a computer screen) to listen.

Above all, don't give up. I hear too often stories of young teachers who become frustrated with the work and wonder if they made the right choice in selecting this career. Think back to why you originally selected teaching, reflect on which moments you have found rewarding and validating and reaffirm teaching as a career for you. In some cases, teaching may not be the best match for your personality, but don't give up immediately because of this kind of frustration.

Keep in mind that stress management is about finding the root causes of stress, identifying your reactions to stress, and then managing that stress and the causes through a preestablished intervention plan. Skipping steps in creating a management plan will not help in the long term and will just create additional problems.

And remember to honor your work, take pride in what you do and know that the stress you feel today may not be with you tomorrow, but the students you work with will hold with them the lasting impact of your care as a teacher.

NOTES

1. Stephanie Paterson, "Four Antidotes for Burnout and Breakdown in the Teaching Life," *The English Record: Reflect, Renew and Revive. Regenerating Our Teaching Selves* 59 (Spring 2009): 3–10.

2. Parker J. Palmer, "The Grace of Great Things: Reclaiming the Sacred in Knowing, Teaching, and Learning," in *The Heart of Learning: Spirituality in Education*, ed. Steven Glazer (New York: Penguin Putnam, 1994), 15–32. Italics in original.

3. Rachel Naomi Remen, "Educating for Mission, Meaning and Compassion," in *The Heart of Learning: Spirituality in Education*, ed. Steven Glazer (New York: Penguin Putnam, 1999), 33–50.

4. Ibid., 37.

5. Ron Miller, "Holistic Education for an Emerging Culture," in *The Heart of Learning: Spirituality in Education*, ed. Steven Glazer (New York: Penguin Putnam, 1994), 189–201.

6. Nel Noddings, "An Ethic of Caring and Its Implications for Instructional Arrangements," in *The Education Feminism Reader*, ed. Lynda Stone (New York and London: Routledge, 1994), 177.

7. Ibid.

8. Parker J. Palmer, *The Courage to Teach* (San Francisco: Jossey-Bass, 1998), 150–56.

9. Ibid., 153.

10. Anjalee Deshpande Nadkarni, "Two Boards and a Passion: On Theatre, Academia, and the Art of Failure," in *Mama, PhD: Women Write about Motherhood and Academic Life*, eds. Elrena Evans and Caroline Grant (New Brunswick, N.J. and London: Rutgers University Press, 2009), 66–71.

About the Author

Kjersti VanSlyke-Briggs is an assistant professor of secondary English education at the State University of New York College at Oneonta. She received her doctorate degree from Binghamton University in New York. Her research interests include literacy and twemty-first-century literacies, caring classrooms, and feminist perspectives in education.

VanSlyke-Briggs is a past president of the New York State English Council. She also taught high school in an alternative school prior to starting a career teaching for Oneonta.

www.ingramcontent.com/pod-product-compliance
Lightning Source LLC
Chambersburg PA
CBHW021822270326
41932CB00007B/293